J R. Richmond
Blanguell, 1960

£3-50

THE PASSIONATE SIGHTSEER

I   Masaccio: 'Tribute Money' (*c.* 1425–7, detail), Santa Maria del Carmine, Florence   ▶

BERNARD BERENSON

The PASSIONATE

SIGHTSEER

from the diaries   *1947 to 1956*

PREFACE BY RAYMOND MORTIMER

168 illustrations in photogravure

3 plates in full colour

 THAMES AND HUDSON · LONDON

Contents

	PAGE
List of Illustrations	6
Photographic Sources	13
Preface	15
Rome May 1947 to June 1955	17
Venice July 1951 to June 1954	37
Sicily May to June 1953	65
Tripoli and Leptis Magna May 1955	129
Calabria June 1955	141
The Romagna September 1955	161
Florence June to July 1956	169
Notes	193
Index	194

List of Illustrations

COLOUR PLATES   FACING PAGE

   I   Masaccio: 'Tribute Money' (*c.* 1425–7, detail), Santa Maria del Carmine, Florence (frontispiece)   3

  II   Apse of Sant'Apollinare in Classe, Ravenna, with the 'Transfiguration' in mosaic (middle of sixth century A.D.)   160

 III   'The Emperor Justinian I with his Suite and Archbishop Maximian', mosaic (middle of sixth century A.D.), San Vitale, Ravenna   161

BLACK-AND-WHITE ILLUSTRATIONS   PAGE

  1   Aqueduct of Claudius (photo *c.* 1880)   17

  2   Distant view of the Vatican and St Peter's (photo *c.* 1880)   18

  3   The Roman Campagna (beginning of the twentieth century)   19

  4   Santa Maria in Cosmedin, Rome   20

  5   Santa Maria Maggiore, Rome   21

  6   Atrium of San Lorenzo fuori le Mura, Rome   22

  7   Temple of Fortune, Palestrina   23

  8   Roman relief (fourth century A.D.), Palazzo Sacchetti, Rome   24

  9   Francesco Salviati: Decorative fresco, Palazzo Sacchetti, Rome   25

 10   The Holy Child, Santa Maria in Aracoeli, Rome   27

 11   After a design by Raphael: Jonah, Santa Maria del Popolo, Rome   28

 12   Tomb of a Princess of the Odescalchi Chigi family, Santa Maria del Popolo, Rome   29

 13   'Life on the Nile', detail of a mosaic, Palestrina Museum   31

 14   Detail of a wall painting from the Villa of Livia, Museo delle Terme, Rome   32

 15   Tepidarium, Baths of Caracalla, Rome   33

 16   Michelangelo: Moses (detail), San Pietro in Vincoli, Rome   35

 17   Cardo degli Aurighi, Ostia   36

18 'The Tower of Babel', mosaic in the atrium, San Marco, Venice 37

19 Cloister at San Francesco del Deserto, Lagoon of Venice 38

20 San Francesco del Deserto, Lagoon of Venice 39

21 Sixteenth-century cloister at San Giorgio Maggiore (Giorgio Cini Foundation), Venice 40

22 Dormitory in the former Monastery, San Giorgio Maggiore (Giorgio Cini Foundation), Venice 41

23 Lorenzo Lotto: 'Miracle of St Clare', fresco, Oratorio Suardi, Trescore 42

24 Lorenzo Lotto: 'Death of Absalom', tarsia, Santa Maria Maggiore, Bergamo 43

25 Lorenzo Lotto: 'St Jerome in the Wilderness', Louvre, Paris 45

26 Francesco di Giorgio: Palazzo del Governo, Iesi 46

27 Santa Casa, Loreto 47

28 Campo San Moisè, Venice, as it was 49

29 Campo San Moisè, Venice, as it is 49

30 Tintoretto: 'Temptation of Christ' (detail), Scuola di San Rocco, Venice 50

31 Tintoretto: 'Christ before Pilate' (detail), Scuola di San Rocco, Venice 51

32 Tintoretto: 'Flight into Egypt' (detail), Scuola di San Rocco, Venice 53

33 Titian: 'Martyrdom of St Lawrence', Gesuiti, Venice 55

34 Cathedral and Santa Fosca, Torcello, Lagoon of Venice 56

35 Interior of Santa Fosca, Torcello, Lagoon of Venice 57

36 Byzantine pilaster and capital, San Marco, Venice 58

37 Side entrance, San Marco, Venice 59

38 'Alexander the Great ascending to Heaven', Byzantine relief, San Marco, Venice 60

39 Porphyry head of a Byzantine Emperor, San Marco, Venice 61

40 Gentile Bellini: Mosaic on the façade of San Marco (detail of 'The Corpus Christi Procession'), Accademia, Venice 62

41 St Luke, detail of the Pala d'Oro, San Marco, Venice 63

42 Façade of the Chiesa dei Minori Osservanti, Palazzolo Acreide 65

43 The Straits of Messina — 66

44 The Sea-front, Messina (before 1908) — 67

45 Montorsoli: Fountain of Orion (1550), Messina — 68

46 Central porch of Messina Cathedral — 69

47 Antonello da Messina: 'Portrait of a Man', Cefalù Museum — 71

48 Antonello da Messina: 'Crucifixion' (detail), Sibiù Museum — 72

49 Antonello da Messina: 'Crucifixion' (1475, detail), Musée Royal, Antwerp — 73

50 Greek Theatre, Taormina — 75

51 Mantegna: 'Agony in the Garden', National Gallery, London — 76

52 General view with the Rocca di Mola, Taormina — 77

53 General view, Agira — 78

54 General view, Centuripe — 79

55 General view of Calascibetta from Enna — 81

56 Head of a horse, detail of a mosaic (fourth century A.D.), Casale — 82

57 Head of a buffalo, detail of a mosaic (fourth century A.D.), Casale — 83

58 After a design by Botticelli: Embroidered cope (detail), Museo Poldi Pezzoli, Milan — 84

59 Embroidered cope, Cathedral Museum (not University), Perugia — 85

60 Female athletes, detail of a mosaic (fourth century A.D.), Casale — 87

61 Francesco Laurana: Eleonora of Aragon, Museo Nazionale, Palermo — 88

62 Francesco Laurana: Madonna (c. 1474), Chiesa dei Minori Osservanti, Palazzolo Acreide — 89

63 Edward Brandard: 'View from Fort Labdalon, Syracuse', engraving — 90

64 Spring of Arethusa, Syracuse — 91

65 Fragment of a laver, Museo Medioevale, Palazzo Bellomo, Syracuse — 92

66 Left aisle of the Cathedral with columns from the Temple of Athena, Syracuse — 93

67 Early Christian sarcophagus, Museo Archeologico, Syracuse — 94

68 Balconies of the Palazzo Villadorato, Noto — 95

69 Cathedral of San Giorgio, Ragusa Ibla — 96

		PAGE
70	Church of San Giorgio, Modica	97
71	Teatro Comunale and Chiesa della Madonna delle Grazie, Vittoria	99
72	John Cousen: 'Temple Area, Agrigento, from the South', engraving	100
73	Arthur Willmore: 'Temple of Concord, Agrigento', engraving	100
74	Limoges casket in the sacristy of Agrigento Cathedral (twelfth century)	101
75	Head of a giant from the Temple of Zeus, Agrigento Museum	102
76	Head of a giant from the Temple of Zeus, Agrigento Museum	102
77	Sarcophagus of Phaedra in the sacristy of Agrigento Cathedral (third century B.C.)	103
78	Altar of the Chthonic Deities, Agrigento	104
79	Peristyle of the Temple of Concord, Agrigento	105
80	Francesco Laurana: Madonna, Sciacca	106
81	Palazzo 'Lo Steripinto', Sciacca	107
82	Kouros from Selinunte, Municipio, Castelvetrano	108
83	Castello, Erice	109
84	Roman sarcophagus with 'Meleager hunting the Calydonian Boar' (second century A.D.), Mazzara del Vallo Cathedral	109
85	John Cousen: 'Distant View of the Temple, Segesta', engraving	110
86	Temple with Monte Varvaro, Segesta	111
87	School of Nino Pisano: Madonna, with ex-votos, Santuario dell'Annunziata, Trapani	112
88	School of Nino Pisano: Madonna, without ex-votos, Santuario dell'Annunziata, Trapani	112
89	Baroque staircase in the former Convent of the Annunziata (Museo Pepoli), Trapani	113
90	Mosaic in Roger's Apartment, Palazzo Reale, Palermo	114
91	Oriental ceiling, Cappella Palatina, Palermo	115
92	Interior of Monreale Cathedral	116
93	Capitals with the 'Annunciation', Cloister of the Benedictines, Monreale	117

94 Capitals with 'William II offering the Church to the Madonna', Cloister of the Benedictines, Monreale · 117

95 'The Rape of Europa', metope from Selinunte, Museo Nazionale, Palermo · 118

96 'Artemis and Actaeon', metope from Selinunte, Museo Nazionale, Palermo · 119

97 'The Triumph of Death' (detail), fresco, Palazzo Abbatelli, Palermo · 120

98 Porphyry socle on the Tomb of Frederick II, Palermo Cathedral · 121

99 Decorative sculptures, Villa Palagonia, Bagheria · 122

100 Chapel of the Villa Palagonia, Bagheria · 123

101 Palazzo della Zisa, Palermo · 124

102 John Cousen: 'View of Old Palermo', engraving · 125

103 Edward Brandard: 'The Old Promenade, Palermo', engraving · 125

104 Entrance to the Grotto of St Rosalia, Monte Pellegrino, Palermo · 127

105 View of Palermo with the Cathedral and Monte Pellegrino · 128

106 Head of Neptune, mosaic, Tripoli Museum · 129

107 Patio, Saniet Volpi, Tripoli · 131

108 Oasis-garden, Saniet Volpi, Tripoli · 131

109 Theatre, Sabratha · 132

110 Great floor mosaic, Sabratha · 133

111 Bernard Berenson in the 'push-cart' at Leptis Magna, escorted by Ernesto Vergara Caffarelli · 134

112 Forum of Septimius Severus, Leptis Magna · 135

113 Basilica of Septimius Severus, Leptis Magna · 135

114 Decorative tendril from a pilaster, Basilica of Septimius Severus, Leptis Magna · 136

115 Theatre, Leptis Magna · 137

116 Arch of Marcus Aurelius, Tripoli · 138

117 Relief from Ghirza (sixth century A.D.), Tripoli Museum · 139

118, 119 Crouching figure in ivory, probably Alexandrine (second century A.D.), Tripoli Museum · 140

120 San Marco, Rossano Calabro · 141

121 Greek wig in bronze (fifth century B.C.), Reggio Museum · 142

122 Greek head in marble (fifth century B.C.), Reggio Museum   143

123 Archaic Greek votive tablet from Locri, Reggio Museum   144

124 Archaic Greek votive tablet from Locri, Reggio Museum   145

125 Edward Lear: 'View of Reggio', lithograph   147

126 Edward Lear: 'View of Scilla', lithograph   148

127 Edward Lear: 'View of Gerace', lithograph   149

128 Gerace Cathedral   150

129, 130 Byzantine enamelled cross, Bishop's Palace, Cosenza   151

131 Head of the Madonna, detail from the Tomb of Isabella of Aragon, Cosenza Cathedral   152

132 Tomb of Isabella of Aragon, Cosenza Cathedral   153

133 Chiesa Madre, Altomonte Calabro   155

134 Santa Maria del Patirion, near Rossano Calabro   156

135 Tomb of Filippo Sangineto, Chiesa Madre, Altomonte Calabro   157

136 Mosaic floor (detail), Santa Maria del Patirion, near Rossano Calabro   159

137 Sant'Apollinare in Classe, Ravenna   161

138 Mosaic in the Mausoleum of Galla Placidia, Ravenna   162

139 Mausoleum of Galla Placidia, Ravenna   163

140 Façade of the Tempio Malatestiano, Rimini   165

141 West wall of the Tempio Malatestiano, Rimini   166

142 Giovanni Boldini: Sketch for a portrait, Museo Boldini, Ferrara   167

143 Giovanni Boldini: Sketch for a portrait, Museo Boldini, Ferrara   167

144 Pomposa Abbey   168

145 Master of the Castello 'Nativity': 'Annunciation', San Giovannino dei Cavalieri, Florence   169

146 Paolo Uccello: 'The Drunkenness of Noah' (detail), detached fresco from the Chiostro Verde, Santa Maria Novella, Florence   170

147 Master of the Castello 'Nativity': 'Miracle of St Benedict', detached fresco from the cloisters of the Badia, Florence   171

148 Master of the Castello 'Nativity': Leading lines under the 'Miracle of St Benedict', Badia, Florence   171

149 Bronzino: 'Laura Battiferri', Loeser Bequest, Palazzo Vecchio, Florence   172

150 Tino di Camaino: Angel, Loeser Bequest, Palazzo Vecchio, Florence   172

151 Sala dei Gigli after restoration, Palazzo Vecchio, Florence   173

152 Studiolo of Eleonora after restoration, Palazzo Vecchio, Florence   175

153 Daniele da Volterra: Bust of Michelangelo, Museo Buonarroti, Florence   176

154 Michelangelo: 'Pietà' (detail), Florence Cathedral   177

155 Masaccio: 'The Holy Trinity with two Donors', fresco, Santa Maria Novella, Florence   179

156 Lorenzo Monaco: 'Marriage of the Virgin' (detail), fresco, Santa Trinita, Florence   180

157 Lorenzo Monaco: 'Nativity of the Virgin' (detail), fresco, Santa Trinita, Florence   180

158 Loggia, Museo Horne, Florence   181

159 Donatello: Cantoria (detail), Opera del Duomo, Florence   182

160 Luca della Robbia: Cantoria (detail), Opera del Duomo, Florence   183

161 Michelangelo: Prisoner, Accademia, Florence   184

162 Michelangelo: 'Palestrina Pietà', Accademia, Florence   185

163 Paolo Uccello: Fragment of a fresco, San Miniato, Florence   186

164 Pulpit, San Miniato, Florence   187

165 Main entrance of the Fortezza del Belvedere, Florence   189

166 Loggia of San Martino alla Palma, Scandicci   190

167 Andrea del Castagno: 'Eve', fresco, Villa Carducci, Legnaia   191

168 Medieval inscription, San Martino alla Palma, Scandicci   192

Photographic Sources

Dr. S. L. Agnello, Syracuse, 62

Alinari, Florence, 11, 12, 20, 25, 26, 27, 30, 41, 43, 44, 45, 46, 61, 65, 67, 77, 83, 101, 104, 156, 157, 158, 159

Anderson, Rome, 4, 5, 10, 13, 15, 16, 18, 31, 33, 36, 39, 47, 50, 51, 78, 90, 91, 93, 94, 95, 96, 98, 105, 137, 138, 139, 144, 160, 164

Assessorato Turismo Siciliano, Palermo, 56

Bazzechi, Florence, 165

Bernard Berenson, Florence, 1, 2, 3, 8, 9, 19, 23, 32, 58, 59, 63, 72, 73, 80, 85, 102, 103, 107, 108, 111, 114, 125, 126, 127, 129, 130, 149, 162, 168

Osvaldo Böhm, Venice, 29, 34, 35, 38, 40

Brogi, Florence, 37, 84, 87, 150, 153, 154, 161

Direzione Civici Musei, Venice, 28

Ente Provinciale Turismo, Ragusa, 69, 70

Ente Provinciale Turismo, Reggio di Calabria, 136

Ente Provinciale Turismo, Trapani, 82

Fondazione Giorgio Cini, Venice, 21

Fototeca Unione, Rome, 6, 7

Gabinetto Fotografico Nazionale, Rome, 17, 49

G. Di Giovanni, Noto, 68

Gino Guisti, Florence, 145

Prof. Max Hirmer, Munich, II, III

Elisabeth Z. Kelemen, Norfolk, Conn., 52, 55, 100

Fosco Maraini, Rome, 79, 92

Maltese, Syracuse, 42

Morettifilm, Rimini, 140, 141

Mostra Antonelliana, Messina, 48

Museo Boldini, Ferara, 142, 143

Museo Civico Archeologico, Agrigento, 74, 75, 76, 81

Museo Pepoli, Trapani, 88, 89

Dr. Alfred Nawrath, Bremen, and Anton Schroll and Co., Vienna, 54, 64, 66, 86, 99

A. Paoletti, Milan, 24

Soprintendenza alle Antichità, Reggio di Calabria, 121, 122, 123, 124, 128

Soprintendenza alle Antichità, Rome, 14

Soprintendenza alle Antichità, Syracuse, 57, 60

Soprintendenza alle Gallerie, Florence, 146, 147, 148, 155, 163, 166, 167

Soprintendenza alle Gallerie della Sicilia, Palermo, 97

Soprintendenza ai Monumenti e Scavi in Libia, Tripoli, 106, 109, 110, 112, 113, 115, 116, 117, 118, 119

Soprintendenza ai Musei Civici, Florence, 151, 152

Stabilimento Poligrafico Alterocca S. A., Terni, 120

Bruno Stefani, Milan, 131, 132, 133, 135

Touring Club Italiano, Milan, 53, 71, 134

Guglielmo Visentini, Venice, 22

To Freya Stark with affectionate admiration

IN 1889, Berenson tells us, Ravenna seemed at the bottom of the sea of time, almost as silent as the grave: a footfall made an echo. Most of the other places in which he kept these diaries had similarly been visited by him sixty-seven years earlier; and by comparing his latest impressions with his first he keeps reminding us of this fact, which is not only singular but relevant. Nobody has ever before written about visual art from so long an experience. Nor indeed can I think of any previous author (except possibly the French philosopher, Fontenelle) who prepared for publication writings composed at the age of ninety-two. Berenson had corrected the proofs of this book when death overtook his delicate frame and persistent curiosity.

'The older I get, the more do I feel and appreciate Botticelli' (of whom he had talked with Pater in person). 'I feel as if it had taken me all these years from 1888 to learn to appreciate Venice fully.' Those whom the gods love do not die young: they live to be old, remaining quick to learn and to feel. But they are few, and need to be wise as well as fortunate.

Our diarist not merely acquired unique experience: he enjoyed it intensely. He made himself a paragon of learning, but he remained first and foremost a voluptuary. 'A rational voluptuary' (I quote Gibbon) 'adheres with invariable respect to the temperate dictates of nature'; and Berenson was not merely rational but fastidious in the extreme. His greed was confined to the pleasures of thinking, of reading, of talking, and above all of using his eyes. What he sought in the arts was the enhancement of life. As an art-historian he explored and mapped the foothills in order to intensify his understanding and enjoyment of the peaks. As these journals make clear, he responded with no less gusto and delicacy to the beauties of nature than to artefacts. A dawn in Taormina brought him 'sheer visual happiness' such as only a Wordsworth could have expressed in words. During the visit to Tripolitania here described I watched with envy his rapturous, physical delight in trees and flowers no less than in the huge majesty of Leptis.

This passion for the visible world underlay his aesthetic preferences and theories. He exalted 'tactile values' in painting, I believe, because they brought beauty as it were within his grasp. Although he wrote the earliest eulogy of Cézanne in English (before this century began) and was among the first champions of Matisse, he rebuked some idolized modern artists—not for lack of talent but for its misuse. He thus, I think regrettably, alienated many who would otherwise relish his writings. The criticism of Picasso (and even of Seurat) may be partly explained by his comments here upon Goethe's blindness to medieval art: 'Even the most gifted of us can never get much beyond what he was taught to understand in his formative years.' But more influential upon his taste was a veneration for the beauties of Nature, and in particular of the human body, which modern painters so often seem to detest.

What Berenson loved best was the art of classical Greece, and after that the art of the Italian Renaissance that pursues a similar end. This might roughly be defined as the golden mean between realism and idealization. The artist creates images of the visible world free from the imperfections by which this is flawed in actuality: Aphrodite and Apollo become more beautiful than any creature without stiffening into idols detached from the flesh. Many of the supreme artists—Byzantine, Romanesque, Chinese, Flemish, Spanish, Dutch, early Italian and nineteenth-century French—have been inspired by aims different from this; and Berenson responded with enthusiasm to their achievements. His collection includes early Chinese bronzes and a number of pictures by the Sienese Primitives. In his youth, however, the Greeks captured his heart once and for all: it leapt whenever he could detect their influence in any work, Roman, Etruscan, Byzantine, even Gothic. Some readers familiar with his research into Trecento painting may be surprised by the relish in these diaries for the Settecento. In his attachment to the classical world he was himself a man of the eighteenth century.

The diaries of a writer so famous everywhere require no preface. But Berenson is sometimes thought of chiefly as an expert unrivalled in his science; and these halting comments may possibly help to correct any such misconception. In any case they are intended above all as a homage to a man infatuated with the beauty of nature and of art.

RAYMOND MORTIMER

1   Aqueduct of Claudius (photo *c.* 1880)

2 Distant view of the Vatican and St Peter's (photo *c.* 1880)

May 7, 1947   I knew a Rome where country not only embraced town but invaded it almost to Piazza di Spagna. From the terrace before San Giovanni in Laterano the fields stretched uncontaminated, with only an ancient wine-shop here and there, to the Sleeping Beauty of the Alban hills. Now the eye beholds the hideous pell-mell of one of the most squalidly pretentious suburbs on the continent. It invades and spoils the solitude of what was the Campagna, and even disturbs the remains of romantic ruins like those on the Via Appia or the Antique tombs of the Porta Latina. The Pyramid of Cestius looks like an ancient dame in a brothel. The asphalted Via Appia has become drearily unevocative.

May 20, 1947   To the Pallavicini Collection, chiefly in order to see the Botticelli again, the woman with head in her hands, seated on a stone bench outside a massive palace with closed doors.[1] Doubtless end of a *cassone*, the other short end of which, as well as sides, have not yet been identified. Once more its drawing, its line, its colour even, its expression of utter abandonment penetrated me to the

18

3 The Roman Campagna (beginning of the twentieth century)

4 Santa Maria in Cosmedin, Rome

depths of the soul. Indeed the older I get the more do I feel and appreciate Botticelli. His art seems to reach the pinnacle of what for me is draughtsmanship, the functional line, the contour that sings, the loveliness of the envelope enclosing shapes so caressingly. His young women can have the tender and appealing charm of the most refined Watteaus but without the least touch of the grisette or the *machine à plaisir*.

May 26, 1947   Santa Maria in Cosmedin restored to aspect of what is supposed to be a Christian basilica of the early Middle Ages. Composed as a *cento* made out of Antique columns, capitals, marble screens of so-called Lombard period, Cosmati floors and pierced windows making a chequered pattern. None of it offends me while the restored frescoes do. Is it then that restorations in my own field distress me because I feel their falsity, and that architect-archaeologists feel the same about restorations in their domain? Scarcely, for in architecture restora-

5 Santa Maria Maggiore, Rome

tions can be made that annoy through over-meticulousness and preconceived schemes and not as in my field where I encounter gross misrepresentations and inferiority of execution. The worst about these restored basilicas is their emptiness, their look as if they served to show off the restorer's skill, rather than to impress as temples of the Lord.

Loafed about Santa Maria Maggiore enjoying the gorgeous space of the nave, the perspective of the columns, the splendour of the great chapels. Surely the magnificence, the sumptuousness of the Roman churches (and to a certain extent and degree of all Italian churches) must inspire those who frequent them with admiration and aspiration without the envy that might be roused if they were being shown a similar display in private palaces. No matter how untaught, people cannot move around in these churches without its influencing their outlook on the universe and without furnishing them with standards and values.

November 2, 1947

6 Atrium of San Lorenzo fuori le Mura, Rome

| November 13, 1947 | Difficult to fathom the satisfaction it gives me to wander about and look and look, in and out of churches, examining everything, every bit of pavement, every sepulchral monument, every bust, every painting. And the ruins, how they fascinate and puzzle me. What did the buildings of which they formed part look like? Is it my imagination that finds in them reminders of a noble past? Are my feelings about them the mere piling up of sentiments and habits of adoration, formed in my earliest years? How *pius* I have been and yet, if I am known at all, it is as a destructive, heartless critic. |

| October 8, 1950 | At San Lorenzo fuori le Mura. Enjoyed the exquisite, crisp, vital carving of Antique fragments as well as of medieval frieze over porch, and the same qualities in the flutings of the columns and the carving of Antique capitals. Is it really life-enhancing in an almost physiological way (as I believe) or merely pleasure in what through use and wont for so many years one has got accustomed to, and one has learned to enjoy or got into the habit of enjoying—the way one enjoys 'mother's cooking' when one returns to it? Perhaps there is a good bit of |

7 Temple of Fortune,
   Palestrina

all that in my enjoyment of the Antique workmanship as well as in the ideated
sensations they convey to me. I enjoy ruins for the same reason and groups of
pell-mell buildings that compose picturesquely.

To the excavations of Palestrina accompanied by an American archaeologist   *October 11, 1950*
and friend. I observed that the vast structure contained elements of different
epochs but he assured me it was built of a piece and on a definite design. He
went on to say that the Latin Cyclopean walls, even those at Alatri, were no

earlier than *circa* 200 B.C. and built in that way for aesthetic reasons. The possibility of such a motive seemed unlikely to me and we concluded that it must have been for magical reasons. The safety of a town may have depended on every stone being of a certain size and trimming, just as in Latin ritual every syllable had to be uttered in such-and-such a way because otherwise it would have lost its power to compel the numen to do its bidding.

October 12, 1950   I know no geometrical shape as perfect as the dome of St Peter's. The least attempt to anthropomorphize it would end in caricature or puerility like turning a human face into a football or seeing a human face in the full moon. (And yet in the Arab-speaking world there is no higher compliment to beauty than to say, 'Her face is like the moon on its fourteenth day'.) I sympathize with the tendency to geometrize objects, including animals and even humans, and approve of a compromise. The real problem, apart from technique, is to find the exact compromise between geometry and representation.

October 25, 1950   To an exhibition of drawings by Seurat. His whole bag of tricks is that his notation—rather like Carrière's—consists of picking objects out of a mist. In Carrière's case it is a real foggy dimness even in interiors, while Seurat seems to see everything through a cheese-cloth or canvas. As a matter of fact, an easy but also a cheap way of getting plastic effects. To hail Seurat as discoverer of

9 Francesco Salviati: Decorative fresco, Palazzo Sacchetti, Rome

form, as a creator of vision, is utterly unjustified. A new or merely unhackneyed notation is not necessarily a new vision. Today some new trick of notation suffices to mark a painter as a great artist.

To Palazzo Sacchetti which I had never visited before. The show-piece a hall frescoed by Salviati. Interesting the Pompeian device of a triptych represented as if hanging like a picture on a wall. Salviati must have seen something like this in Rome, for Pompeii, where frescoes of that type occur so often, was still buried and undreamt of. Most interesting also, on the entrance floor a Roman relief which architecturally is of the fourth century while the figures decidedly recall earlier centuries.[2]

October 29, 1950

25

October 31, 1950   I first came to Rome in the autumn of 1888 and spent the following months on my feet from early morning till bedtime. *Caffè latte* cost me five soldi. Often had no lunch but munched chestnuts and found them very comforting, and in my pocket they warmed my hands. Used to dine at the Concordia with a lot of jolly Scandinavians like Christian Ross, and an Englishman, Mr Davies. I slept in the studio of an acquaintance who rented a trestle bed to me. Except for this group of artists I knew nobody, nor did it occur to me to want to know anybody. Looking was enough and reading, but mostly looking. Here, as in Paris and London, I lived more inwardly than outwardly, although I was active enough. What went on inside me, not always perceived by me, counted as real and satisfactory.

November 6, 1950   At the Aracoeli, fascinated by a chapel crowded with fervent worshippers of an infant Osiris, a baby face, the rest of it all covered in sparkling jewels. I love dolls. The bedizening of this one appealed to the child in me. I am aware of what is going on in me, and know that my feeling is artistic, playful. But the worshippers—are they not, unbeknown to themselves, inspired by similar feelings, perhaps even to a greater extent? Since every manner of thing has been explored and pedantized, no doubt German writers have published tome upon tome on the psychology of religious worship. None have come my way. I would like to write about it from my own experience of long ago, still bright in my memory.

October 18, 1952   In the heroic and court ages people were entertained by 'solemn music', by a definite ritual, be it lay or ecclesiastic and artists knew what was expected from them. Not so today. Entertainment is reduced either to mere time-killing or to the excitement of novelty, to the craving for otherness. Nevertheless these are the only arts still alive for which there is a positive demand and that offer great rewards. Witness the cinema and the songster of the day who hits the public on its funny-bone. Cheap, shoddy, journalistic as they are they yet are real, answer to a real need, to something craved for. They may serve as soil and humus for genius, while there is at present nothing to be hoped for from the activities of most visual artists with their denial of their own art, which has always been and always will be of representation and not (except incidentally) of abstraction.

October 27, 1952   Drove yesterday from Piazza Venezia to Palazzo Taverna on Monte Giordano. Could recognize familiar objects as we passed them and the distance seemed the usual one. From Palazzo Taverna to Piazza del Popolo along the dimly-lit Tiber the distance seemed endless. Was it because I could not make out at every step just where we were? Our sense of distance would seem to depend on

10 The Holy Child,
Santa Maria in Aracoeli, Rome

the succession of details. If we recognize only few of them the distance seems longer, and vice versa shorter. Exact parallel with time. Quick succession of events makes duration seem short while a slow succession, or very rare events, makes time seem longer and no events makes it seem endless. Therefore, when there will be no events time will cease although duration will last and remain unchanged. In short, time is a human notion.

November 2, 1952

I understand why I dislike innovation that comports removal or out-and-out destruction of buildings that I have got used to, of streets to which I had not only visually but muscularly got habituated. But why should I be distressed that the future will not miss them? Perhaps it is that we attach our own survival (in a measure at least) to things looking the way we have known them and that we die again with their disappearance and their replacement with other things that our ghosts could not recognize? Ghosts are seldom of more than two, or at most three generations back, unless they become spooks as perhaps Nero did for centuries.

November 7, 1952

An hour in Santa Maria del Popolo. Poked about in corridors, sacristies, closets, as well as in the church itself. What variety! Early and late Renaissance tombs, two of them done by the incumbent in his lifetime. They knew better than to trust their heirs. Choir with ceiling by Pinturicchio at his best, and tombs by Andrea Sansovino anticipating schemes adopted later by Michelangelo for the sepulchre of Julius II at San Pietro in Vincoli. The chapel with frescoes by Pinturicchio again at his best; the recumbent bronze by Vecchietta, the two Caravaggios placed in such a way as to suggest that those who ordered them did not think too highly of them. The charming Jonah in the Chigi

Chapel delighted me again. But what impressed me most this time was the
tomb of an Odescalchi lady, who died at twenty-two in her third childbirth,
made in 1772 or thereabouts. That such a masterpiece, rivalling the best Chinese
art for expression of energy in leaves, in the eagle, the tree trunk, the sweep of
the drapery, not to speak of the colour, had been done so late, only just before
the collapse into the 'art nouveau' which we know as 'Empire', amazed me.

12 Tomb of a Princess of the Odescalchi Chigi family, Santa Maria del Popolo, Rome

November 16, 1952	The Campidoglio, its palaces, the Forums, the Colosseum, floodlit are fascinating, if garish. Fascinating to see the shapes in unusual light. This satisfies our demand for 'otherness', our childish pleasure in the out of the way. Floodlighting certainly displays effects, angles, facets, which do not show up so emphatically in daylight. It acts in the nature of a comment, an interpretation, a fresh and perhaps revealing aspect of the workaday sunlit appearance of things. For myself I soon have enough of it, as I quickly tire of attempts to show up, for instance, Michelangelo's sculpture in photography from angles and points of view never contemplated by the artist. The normal is what daylight reveals when we stand more or less parallel with an object and look at it. All the rest is an amusing and possibly interesting diversion.
November 19, 1952	When unoccupied as in matutinal insomnia or when obliged to wait expecting to do something or to catch a train the next minute, time seems endless, as if jellified instead of flowing. On the other hand, if one is pleasantly acting as in creative work or travelling, or of course enjoying every kind of life-enhancing human contact, time seems to rush along. Yet when one looks back, time that one suffered almost vanishes from memory while time enjoyed gets more and more extended the more and more one succeeds in recalling the events that constitute it. What then is time? Eventless duration or what? No doubt it has been pondered over, discussed and written about for thousands of years but either I have not read any of it or have forgotten. For me at least time is largely subjective—in that respect unlike space which is concrete, definite, the same for all, no matter how swiftly or slowly one traverses it, and space is reversible whereas time is not. And yet space itself has a subjective element, despite measurable distance. Here in Via Ludovisi I am literally a stone's throw from Via Sistina and sixty years ago it would have seemed no distance at all. Now it does. It used to seem nothing to walk from the Trinità dei Monti to St Peter's, to the Colosseum, to the end of the monument-lined part of the Via Appia. Now they are distances out of conceivable reach. As a matter of fact, I now measure space not in terms of distance but in terms of fatigue.
November 24, 1952	All arts used to be aspirational. Few now are. One of them is the ballet which perhaps is the reason why, like fairy stories, it pleases little ones as much as grown-ups. The ballet gives us spectacles of men and women as beautiful as we should like to be, as agile and able to use their limbs. It is limited and made monotonous by the fact that we have but two legs and two arms and a limited number of twists of neck and turns of head. The Hindus may have tried to rebel against these drawbacks by giving their gods many legs and arms, but as these cannot free themselves more from their bodies than the two legs and

13 'Life on the Nile',
detail of a mosaic,
Palestrina Museum

arms the result is multiple monotony. But with all its drawbacks the ballet is a fairy world, a world where wishful dreaming is fulfilled, if only for the brief moment that we admire it.

At the Museo delle Terme where the great polychrome mosaic from Palestrina is now admirably shown.[3] The chiaroscuro representation of life on the Nile in it is almost modern. Am more impressed than ever by the fecundity of inventiveness and the mastery of artisanship in the Antique down to the middle of our

November 25, 1952

third century. There are Antique objects which we scarcely look at: they would rank high if we took them for works of the fourteenth, fifteenth and sixteenth centuries. In the field of sculpture or mere stone carving Donatello alone among Renaissance artisans can be compared with the Antique average. Artisanship in all fields down to the end of our third century retained a high standard of quality and never became relaxed and flabby, as happens almost universally in contemporary art. Today a painter or sculptor begins by feeling that he has a mission, needs no training in the use of his tools, and must only give vent to his genius by sheer wishful thinking and metaphysicizing.

The so-called 'Garden of Livia' has been brought to the Museo delle Terme *June 28, 1953* and placed in a room of the same size and height as the one it was made for. How dewy, how penetratingly fresh the grass and trees and flowers, how coruscating the fruit. Pomegranates as Renoir painted them. Bird songs charm one's ears. The distance in the 'Garden of Livia' room remains magically impenetrable, veiled as it was in the gardens in Lithuania, where I lived when I first came to awareness. And then the drawing of each leaf in the foreground, with its spiky edge!

After many years returned to the Baths of Caracalla, now bereft of all picturesqueness, of every effort of nature to absorb into its bosom what man has done in competition with her. Now the ruin stands out bare and stark, but how bold, how sublime and still overpoweringly impressive. Those colossal masses of brick, how were they roofed, if roofed at all? How were they finished, stuccoed, decorated? Was the effect better (no matter how much bigger) than interiors in the classical style put up in the last century and that still can be enjoyed in Italian Atlantic liners? Ruins have the advantage of suggesting romantic wishful

November 9, 1953

15 Tepidarium, Baths of Caracalla, Rome

reconstructions, free from disturbing detail and probably bad taste. I doubt whether Karnak or Baalbek were anything like as evocative and satisfactory to tastes like mine when they were going concerns. They may have seemed heavy, pompous, and pretentious.

November 10, 1953 In my younger years the Sistine Chapel was so accessible from the Bernini staircase to the north of St Peter's. The present arrangement is all but inhuman, and must be due to some bureaucratic convenience based on procuring the greatest inconvenience to the greatest number. Miles to walk, stairs to climb up and down, through corridors lined with artifacts that attract attention and strain your energies before you have managed to reach the Sistine Chapel. Tired out by this endless walk and annoyed by herds of tourists bellowed at by guides, I have a very poor impression of the frescoes and cannot get over it. The best Botticellis are on the outer wall where the sun prevents one seeing them. The ceiling looks dark, gloomy. The 'Last Judgment' even more so. What would a dilettante, unacquainted with the subjects of these designs or their iconography, get out of them? A Hindu or Muslim might conclude that admiration for these frescoes was part of the Christian cult and had little to do with art. How much traditional admiration still influences us; how difficult to make up our minds that these Sistine frescoes are nowadays scarcely enjoyable in the original and much more so in photographs.

November 26, 1953 As a child I was fascinated by the story that Moses had horns on his forehead and that they shone with their own light. Indeed in most representations we see no horns but beams of light from his head. Michelangelo in the mighty icon of San Pietro in Vincoli gives him, as a sculptor should, real horns. I wonder whether the tradition does not go back to the fact that he had mighty protuberances on his forehead such as gorillas and Neanderthal humans have? If that could be assumed it would point to the historicity of Moses. A peculiarity of that kind could scarcely have formed part of the ideal law giver, and surely would not form part of the Moses legend, if the peculiarity had not been there visible to all, rousing remarks, and thus was handed down through the ages and gradually became transfigured into rays of light.

November 30, 1953 I have paid twenty visits to the illuminated manuscripts exhibition at Palazzo Venezia and what have I carried away? Only a vague feeling of how much there is to study. To master them artistically and philologically would take a lifetime. So it is with all my travels. The first time I go to an unusual place, the Scandinavian lands, North Africa, Egypt, the Near East, the utmost I carry away is an idea of what to see and what to study on my next visit. But there

34

16 Michelangelo: Moses (detail), San Pietro in Vincoli, Rome

has been no second visit. Long ago I concluded that all we did on earth (no matter how long we lived) was to decide what topics we should pursue if we had eternity at our disposal, with time for everything, no haste, no interest treading on the heels of the last interest. Now I never get over feeling like a charlatan if anything I say is taken too seriously by others.

June 24, 1955   To Ostia, with the last afternoon light of a golden day radiant on the brick walls. What living Claudes, or better still Hubert Roberts, Corots even. How I should have loved to muse there, unaware of strolling, lost in the dream world evoked by 'Landscape with Ruins'. How many I have enjoyed in every part of the Mediterranean world and how eager I am to enjoy them all again with body and soul. Body giving out, will not serve soul, the which more and more restricted in a diminishing circle, leaving no choice but dreams unrealized.

    18 'The Tower of Babel', mosaic in the atrium, San Marco, Venice

July 7, 1951   The Venetian painters and sculptors and architects were my first love but Venice itself, *Venise la ville*, not so much. Now it is the town that fascinates and rejoices me at every step and in all effects of light and, I may say, in almost all weather. And I have come full circle about its painters. Again they appeal to me not only as the most pictural but as the most classical. Classical in the sense in which Greek art from the fifth to the first century is classical—sweetly reasonable, calm in deep feeling and wholly free from rhetoric in the fifteenth century. Sublime with Titian at his best; and imaginative as illustration, by which I mean poetically interpretative, in Tintoretto. Then the Palladian architecture and Longhena and Tiepolo and his precursors way back to the most classical of all, Paolo Veronese.

July 9, 1951   I began my career as an attributor of Italian pictures in Venice and reviewing it I realize that in the first years only did I enquire what others thought and toe the mark after Morelli. After that, documented and dated works were my only stepping stones across the vague lands of connoisseurship. I never consulted authorities, I never thought of disagreeing over an attribution because a contemporary had just made it. Of course many of my own attributions had been anticipated by others. In the case of Giorgione, for instance, it is almost impossible not to have been anticipated seeing that every romantic early sixteenth-

19 Cloister at
San Francesco del Deserto,
Lagoon of Venice

20 San Francesco del Deserto, Lagoon of Venice

century Venetian painting has at one time been attributed to him. When I ascribed the old woman 'Col Tempo' to Giorgione, which to my knowledge at the time nobody had dreamt of giving to him, an American student pointed out that some obscure writer generations ago had already made the same attribution.

Yesterday by motor boat to San Francesco del Deserto. Cinema people were *July 10, 1951* making a documentary, desecrating and vulgarizing what had been so spirit-ually ecstatic. Friars were mowing hay in the meadows and looked as beautiful in colour and action as in Japanese pictures of Buddhist monks. In the *clausura* a fine cloister and beyond it a garden with two tufted palms just as in a Lazzaro

21   Sixteenth-century cloister at San Giorgio Maggiore (Giorgio Cini Foundation), Venice

Bastiani, and a sort of ruined pagoda all overgrown with leafage and topped with red flowers. It shelters two ageless grey tree stumps said to be remains of a tree planted by St Francis himself. With a touch here and there Chinese carvers could have turned these venerable relics into works of art.

October 3, 1953   Whom does a show like the one of Lotto serve? For the public there is far too much of no interest or aesthetic delight. For the *buon gustaio* too many indifferent pictures. Only the so-called art historians, that is the picture attributors, can profit by such an attempt at exhibiting the painting of an artist as uneven as Lotto. And how difficult it is to display them!

Seen out of the penumbral light of the altars and in the light of common day, the Bergamo altarpieces, facing each other and, as it were, lighting each other up, make a poor impression as of rustic over-gaiety of colour. Then there are too many pictures and portraits shown only to induce attributors to find solutions. Yet one cannot but recognize and praise the effort made by Professor Zampetti and his staff, under the auspices of the Biennale, in gathering such a large number of Lotto's paintings and having them properly cleaned and restored.

22 Dormitory in the former Monastery, San Giorgio Maggiore (Giorgio Cini Foundation), Venice

Taken over to the Isle of San Giorgio Maggiore by Count Cini and amazed to *October 6, 1953* see the progress made since I was there two years ago when Nino Barbantini, Cini's chief adviser in the carrying out of this grandiose plan, was still alive and walked around with us. I remember being very much struck then by the resemblance between the original monastic intention and the idea of turning these monumental buildings into a cultural and civic institution. In the new Middle Ages into which we are plunging we again shall need quasi-monastic institutions to save and advance civilization. And by civilization I always mean the effort to humanize mankind and to provide the proper conditions, the best attainable for that purpose. Perhaps in the darkling, noisy, hammering, bombing, warring world into which we already are plunged such neo-monastic establishments may play the part that they had for centuries in our past and in a real sense continued to have until a couple of hundred years ago. Only they will have to acquire a more suitable theology or a new mythology of purpose. What still seemed a somewhat vague plan a few years ago has been realized in an almost miraculous fashion. We walked through the cloisters, up Longhena's grand staircase, through splendid halls for conferences, and vast corridors, spacious reading and sitting rooms, delightful apartments for visiting scholars, a noble library, a nunnery, a trade school and playground for proletarian boys, another for orphans of sailors, an open theatre and a charming indoor one. The elegance of the past is harmonized with the comfort of the present. *Freude am Ursache sein* must be at the bottom of much that is undertaken and naturally the sense of freedom that is given by being able to carry out an intention. Both these elements must dominate in the successful Faustian. What more life-enhancing than to be free to achieve all that, to be master and creator and ordainer. I felt this Faustian quality in Vittorio Cini as he was taking me around. He lives for this creation and nothing makes him happier than to show and to explain it to one whom he believes able to appreciate it.

October 7, 1953 The crowds at the Lotto show appear more interested and freer from boredom than I had expected. I should like to urge every single visitor not to forget the importance of Bergamo and its surroundings in relation to this show and not to miss above all seeing Lotto's fascinating designs for the intarsias at Santa Maria

23 Lorenzo Lotto:
'Miracle of St Clare', fresc
Oratorio Suardi, Trescore

24 Lorenzo Lotto: 'Death of Absalom', tarsia, Santa Maria Maggiore, Bergamo

Maggiore nor the delightful frescoes at Trescore and Credaro. As I wander about comparing one picture to the other, looking at the details of Lotto's enchanting genre scenes and landscapes I am continually reminded of my early days when I first fell in love with this quaintly sensitive painter and decided to study him thoroughly. The pictures that first attracted me and started me off on my pursuit were the so simple and sweetly affectionate family group in the

National Gallery, London, with the ample seascape in the background, the bride and bridegroom in the Prado with its subtle touches of humour, and the exquisite small St Jerome in a romantic landscape at the Louvre.

October 8, 1953 As a youngster of twenty-two I approached a work of art with reverent receptivity, with longing to feel it, appreciate it and understand it. As for Lotto, I went on pilgrimage after pilgrimage with an almost medieval pilgrim's difficulties anywhere and everywhere, no matter what season and what weather, to see a picture in a church of remote and difficult access. On the way I got more eager, zestful, got into a state of grace toward the picture I was hoping to see. As I left it I was filled with its image and had the leisure to absorb it, to make it unforgettably my own. After three or four years of living with and for Lotto I had him in memory as no bringing together of all his output under one roof could have done, for all the while I was unconsciously assimilating, and as unconsciously eliminating and relating and producing the composite image that ends by appearing when I pronounce the name 'Lotto'. I had few reproductions nor did I need them, I remembered and recalled the pictures so vividly.

October 9, 1953 Without losing the fervour of the pilgrim, I soon acquired the zest of the sportsman, of the pioneer and adventurer, the feeling of the Spanish conquistadores who discovered and first looked at the Pacific. Where a Lotto was to be found or seen there I went, regardless of wind and rain, cold and discomfort. Transport sixty-five years ago was reduced to the rickety, slow, overcrowded *corriere* which I never took. I walked when possible or hired a *carozzella* or even a *baghere* and little was the luggage I brought along. In the remotest villages of the Marches there was often nothing to eat but hard bread, onions and anchovies but every morning I awoke to a glamorous adventure, tasted the freshness of a spring or autumn morning in a Bergamesque valley as if it were a deliciously invigorating draught. Each altarpiece in its place in the cool or warm, but penumbral light of a church and its sanctuary atmosphere I enjoyed like the satisfaction of a vow and it remained fixed in memory as a crystalline individuality and not as a mere particle in the *œuvre* of a painter. Its overtones lingered in recollection and its taste on the palate.

October 10, 1953 How different all this from seeing the whole of a master's surviving output, good, bad or indifferent, brought together in crowded rooms without the light and space necessary for their appreciation and even deprived of their raiment: the frame which, I forget what French painter of the last century said, was a reward earned by a good picture (as for me, any frame is better than no frame).

25 Lorenzo Lotto: 'St Jerome in the Wilderness', Louvre, Paris

Indeed in the Middle Ages and Renaissance the frame was as highly considered and cost as much as the painting itself. Now there is a mania for exhibiting pictures, as the Bellinis four years ago, like corpses wrapped in grave cloths, or as in the Lotto exhibition, shivering, naked against chilly gray backgrounds.

October 11, 1953   And what interesting and amusing human contacts the search for Lotto gave me with scholars passionately devoted to the study of the art and history of their town. First among them, Pietro Giannuizzi of Loreto who discovered Lotto's diary just in time for me to use it for my book on that master. Then I remember Canon Giovanni Annibaldi of Iesi who saved the fascinating St Lucy Altarpiece and other Lottos in that town from neglect and published documents about them; the director of the *Rivista Misena*, Anselmi; and the designer and creator of the Vittorio Emmanuele monument in Rome, Giuseppe Sacconi. At Iesi I could enjoy not only the paintings but the majestically massive palace designed by Francesco di Giorgio, perhaps the most many-sided Italian after Leonardo, and I delighted in recalling that just here in the Piazza *coram populo*

26 Francesco di Giorgio:
Palazzo del Governo, Iesi

27 Santa Casa, Loreto ▶

under a sumptuous tent was brought to birth the babe, the *Puer Apuliae*, destined to be the *Stupor Mundi*, one of the most dazzling figures in history, the Hohenstaufen emperor Frederick II.

October 12, 1953   One of the centres for excursions I frequented most was Macerata, a provincial town which in the eighteenth century owed its importance to being a half-way station between Bologna and Rome. I was amused to discover that a colony of English people, for reasons of economy or health, found it convenient to sojourn there. I recall vividly the Giulia of the inn at Macerata who used to prepare succulent evening meals when I returned after a hard day of sightseeing in towns and villages in the neighbourhood. There was a company of engineers at a round table and the sparring that went on between them and her kept us merry. I was surprised to hear such sound notions of economy and politics discussed and to meet even a lively interest in my own pursuits. Giulia was a real *mulier fortis* of the Bible and while not having the gracefulness of Goldoni's Locandiera she reminded me of her in the freedom of her speech and the quickness of her response.

Lotto means all that to me, an integral and unforgettable part of my youth when hope was a breeze laden with happy expectations. I wrote about him to the best of my ability. I am as proud of nothing in my past as of the fact that, although I was adoring him, in my book about the Venetian painters I only mentioned him briefly and never so lost my sense of values as to equate him with Titian or Tintoretto.

October 15, 1953   Wherever I go the subject passionately discussed is the plan of the American architect Lloyd Wright for a *palazzina* to be built on the Canal Grande, just where it makes a curve, so that it would be visible from a long way off. Yesterday I was shown a photo of the project. It looked to me a rather amusing, playful affair, as if copied from one of the Neapolitan painter Monsù's architectural pictures, suitable for a table lantern or even for a pavilion in a suburban public garden, but not for a conspicuous site on the Grand Canal of Venice. It may be argued that many other buildings already line it that should not be there, some of them vulgar eye-sores. Granted, but they do not fall conspicuously out of pattern, nor would any school of bright young architects insist on our admiring them, which they certainly would do before this creation of a romantic and fanciful genius. The most distressing and inharmonious innovations happen not to be on the Canal Grande but elsewhere. Hitherto public areas had been held sacred. Nobody had the temerity to usurp one square foot of them. On the once so delightful Campo San Moisè a bulky, protruding, vast structure has been allowed to go up thereby nearly hiding one of the finest medieval towers.

Chiesa di San Moisè
Architettura di Allesandro Tremignon.

28 Campo San Moisè,
Venice, as it was

29 Campo San Moisè,
Venice, as it is

Not in Venice alone have these usurpations of sky-space, if not of earth-space, been permitted. My thoughts fly to Florence where the approaches to the Ponte Vecchio are now so painful to an eye like mine that I do all I can to avoid them.

Had the late lamented Mussolini lived to be the Augustus of his ambitions he would have left little of medieval and Renaissance Rome. All would have been sacrificed to the pressing needs of traffic.

These needs are the greatest enemies to the beauty of Italy's most famous towns. Laid out and built when even horse vehicles were barely beginning to be

31   Tintoretto:
'Christ before Pilate' (detail),
Scuola di San Rocco, Venice

used, their frequently narrow and tortuous thoroughfares serve now with difficulty for automobiles driven by people crazy for speed. It is a problem demand-
ing patience, tact and taste.

Scuola di San Rocco. Sumptuous, magnificent, spacious this club-house of a   *May 18, 1954*
Venetian guild. As for Tintoretto's paintings, they compare with Rembrandt
for interpretation and as craftsmanship. In one composition, the 'Christ before
Pilate', he surpasses all other artists who have attempted the same theme. In the

'Temptation' Satan is a combination of grossness, impudence and challenging arrogance. The landscapes are among the most romantic ever created, evocative, transporting, nostalgic. In brief, Tintoretto here is as great an illustrator as painting has produced. His colour now is rich and strange, yet satisfying. When these paintings left his hands, they were as dazzling, fresh and radiant as Renoir, as we can see in a bit that was folded back and thus saved from sun and dirt. I am not sure that I don't prefer them toned and mellowed to the condition they are in now.

May 22, 1954   At the Fenice to hear Gieseking play Beethoven. In the intervals the murmur of the crowd filling the theatre sounded like nothing human or even animal. It was like the muted roar of breakers on a rocky shore, and the applause like the vitreous crash of a cataract. If I could not see and did not know I should not have expected that the sounds that reached my ears were made by human beings. Pity I did not think of this when I wrote *Seeing and Knowing*. I could have paralleled it with *Hearing and Knowing*. Looking down from the *loge* I saw blobs of flesh colour and dabs of many other colours that would not have led me to guess they were faces and figures of humans. More and more do I become aware of how much antecedent knowing was injected into seeing, hearing, and smelling as well.

May 24, 1954   Meeting many of my colleagues here makes me think of how until not long ago, when they were taken to an island to run wild and devour each other or starve, the dogs of Constantinople were strictly divided into quarters. Woe to the one who strolled into, let alone tried to occupy another than his own quarter. It is the same with scholars today. I, for instance, am a dog accredited to write on fourteenth- to sixteenth-century Italian painting. Any other publications of mine are resented, attacked or ignored—my *Caravaggio* by nearly all *seicentisti*, my *Aesthetics and History* by all writers on Aesthetics, likewise my *Seeing and Knowing*, my *Arch of Constantine* by all archaeologists. I myself do not exactly resent but severely notice books by students of other periods and schools who butt in with books on Italian artists of my period. I scarcely consider worth-while writings like Malraux's on art although he says much that a gifted out-sider may see in art, while regarding it as mere content and illustration.

May 26, 1954   I feel as if it had taken me all these years, from 1888 until now, to learn to appreciate Venice fully. I may not say that for I have no doubt that if I remain really alive I shall probably appreciate it more and more. Now I even enjoy the crowd in the *calli* and in the Piazza and Piazzetta. Yesterday at seven, with light nearly level with the horizon, walked to the Point of the Dogana and watched

32 Tintoretto:
'Flight into Egypt' (detail),
Scuola di San Rocco, Venice

the flush, the glow on the Doge's Palace, on San Giorgio. It thrilled me when I first saw it, but with vague and turbid understanding. Now I can free it, liberate it, objectivate it, express it even—no longer is it a state of pregnancy but of happy delivery.

The eminent American sociologist, Thorstein Veblen, invented the phrase 'conspicuous waste'. It does not need definition for it rages nowadays and not in the United States only.

But in Venice you float along canals, mere ditches, so narrow that you have to crane your neck to see the edifices on each side. As often as not they have noble proportions and the windows are partitioned with columns of extreme elegance, crowned by stone capitals carved to look like soft cushions of violets and moss.

Why this inconspicuous waste? Few as they passed under them would look up to admire and envy. Possibly because others built as magnificently in more favoured sites and the owners would not be outdone. More probably because, given the outlay, there were no architects, builders, carvers who could do less well. All had been taught and trained in a tradition and practice that admitted neither freaks nor scampings; for each took pride and had pleasure in giving his best, thereby realizing his highest self.

May 28, 1954 High mass yesterday at St Mark's with Cardinal Spellman officiating. Floor and galleries crowded. I stood for a whole hour carried away by the performance, the place. The interior of St Mark's looked more beautifully, more radiantly, also more completely Byzantine than ever. All my senses, sight and sound, were ravished and my mind as well. This appeal, this aspiration, this ecstacy carried me away all the more so as the music, whether of the performers or of the congregation, was unprofessional enough to seem utterly spontaneous. At the end Cardinal Spellman mounted the pulpit, not to preach a sermon but to talk about himself and his joy in officiating in St Mark's and his love for Venice and for Italy. His accent in Italian was not American but distinctly English. It amused me to think that the head of the Irish community in the USA, whose chief objective is the ruin of England, could not help betraying by his accent his indebtedness to England.

May 29, 1954 Yesterday evening a boat-load of Neapolitan musicians singing 'Funiculì Funiculà' and other Neapolitan songs I used to hear when first in Venice in September–October 1888. The boat gaily lit up, followed by gondolas festooned with Japanese lanterns transporting American tourists. For them this nocturnal fantasia is an integral part of Venice and perhaps for many all they will remember of their visit. Indeed, what do the tourists, now travelling not as individuals but in parties, carry away from their two, or at most three days' visit to a town like this? There is the story of the elderly woman whose daughter could not make her recall Venice until, in despair, she asked, 'But, Ma, don't you remember the place where we got the five-button gloves?'

June 12, 1954 Titian's 'Martyrdom of St Lawrence', one of the most romantic representations ever painted—dark night lit up by torches and by the blaze under the gridiron, the beautiful nude of the saint tossing about on it, the columns of the temple looming dimly lit, spectrally discernible, all go to producing an effect at once grandiose and sublime. As a study in light and shade unsurpassed. Caravaggio may, in fact must have seen it and been impressed by it. Yet, at the show of that painter's works, Cremonese precursors were exhibited but not this source of all later chiaroscuro experiments. Had the organizers of the show never seen this

33 Titian:
'Martyrdom of St Lawrence',
Gesuiti, Venice

34 Cathedral and Santa Fosca, Torcello, Lagoon of Venice

Titian at the Gesuiti or did they deliberately ignore it, in opposition to the thesis that Caravaggio owed nearly all to the Venetians? As for the Cremonese, what were they too but imitators of Titian and his chiaroscuro?

June 20, 1954 On balcony this morning between 4.15 and 4.45, flat quiet light, mother-of-pearl tone with touches here and there of rose in the sky. Water oily, seemed to be flowing in but drift went the other way. The Salute like an engraving, or rather an etching, Whistlerish. Watched the gradual lighting up until I was too tired to wait for the full sunlight illuminating the entire sky. Giovanni Bellini and his immediate followers painted skyscapes as if they did them at dawn, probably because they realized the impossibility of doing sunshine. They paint the pallid sunless sky in the evocative way that delights us in even such mediocrities as Basaiti or Bissolo. In Bellini himself the skies are always of pale dawn, except in the Berlin 'Resurrection' where he gives us a sky with crimson cloudlets that revive us and inspire us with a fellow feeling for Him who rose from the dead as triumphant as the sun over the darkness.

June 24, 1954 As I look back on my first visits to Torcello I recall that what I enjoyed and still enjoy is not the archaeological interest of the architecture and the mosaics but the

atmosphere, as at Ravenna, only more poignantly, as if time, having reabsorbed all that had been done so long ago, now reigned calm, soothing, like a cradle song, all so remote because there is no in-between. Today, with eight centuries of events behind us of which nothing remains except two churches, the basilica and the round church with its circumambulatory, one vaguely, dimly dreams of what these buildings meant to those who put them up, whence came what they took for granted must be built, of the great likeness of the round structure

to buildings we have seen in the Hauran and elsewhere in the Near East. All goals of the flights of imagination that make up what I feel at Torcello.

June 25–28, 1954 Art histories and serious guide-books call St Mark's in Venice overwhelmingly Byzantine. I am not sure to what extent the cultivated public has taken in and made its own the significance of San Marco. Not only is it entirely Byzantine, despite later ornamental accretions, but it is the most typical, the most complete and the most satisfactory Byzantine edifice now in existence.

38 'Alexander the Great ascending to Heaven', Byzantine relief, San Marco, Venice

The learned say that it is an exact copy of the Church of the Apostles at Constantinople which was destroyed by Sultan Mohammed II the Conqueror, and rebuilt as a mosque known as Fatimieh, with the excuse that the Church of the Apostles was tottering and dangerously in ruins. A stronger reason for this vandalism was, I suspect, that the ambulatories of the Church of the Apostles sheltered the sarcophagi of the Christian emperors and could fan patriotism like St Denis in France.

In calling San Marco the most complete Byzantine edifice I do not except St Sophia, which makes scarcely any aesthetic appeal on the outside. Inside, St Sophia is no doubt more breath taking as space, but less harmonious, and in its present God abandoned state it has become a dreary, cold museum. Its interior rejoices us with its porphyry columns, their marvellous and varied capitals, and the exquisite wainscoting. In other respects it is now forbiddingly empty. One can scarcely imagine what it may have been like in the great days when it was the cathedral, not of a diocese, but of a vast empire.

San Marco is excitingly rich outside as inside. The bare, naked structure is scarcely visible from Piazza or Piazzetta. One must look for it from within the courtyard of the Doge's Palace, or round the back from the Canal and through

39 Porphyry head
of a Byzantine Emperor,
San Marco, Venice

40 Gentile Bellini: Mosaic on the façade of San Marco (detail of 'The Corpus Christi Procession'), Accademia, Venice

the free passage to the sacristy. Wherever you descry the design and the brick masonry, you perceive an unadulterated Byzantine structure. Within, the raw bones of the structure lie hidden under every kind of Byzantine panelling of varied marbles, within columns of porphyry and other rare stones, some with capitals as of plaited straw, others as of daintily patterned bronze, still others like tops of windswept pine trees, all brought from the Byzantine world if not from Constantinople itself. They not only cluster in the embrasures of the three main entrances but stand free to right and left of the inner doors of the atrium.

The facade and sides, particularly the northern one, are covered over with early and late Byzantine reliefs representing subjects and features, sacred and profane. Even the rare Byzantine-Sassanian motive of Alexander the Great's ascent into heaven is among them. They form a compendious collection of Byzantine sculpture. On the south-west corner of the balcony there is a fine museum piece in the shape of a porphyry head of a Byzantine emperor who, during a rebellion, had his nose cut off. On the south side there are the two groups of the Emperor Diocletian and his imperial colleagues embracing each other. To enumerate these sculptures one by one, outside and inside the basilica, to describe and date them, would fill a bulky catalogue. Has it ever been properly done?

The mosaics above the balcony, except for the one on the extreme left, have

41 St Luke, detail of the Pala d'Oro, San Marco, Venice

disappeared. We find them reproduced in Gentile Bellini's painting of the Corpus Christi procession at the Accademia, as they still existed at the end of the fifteenth century. If there were the will to put them back, it would not be difficult to do so.

Of the mosaics inside the basilica the best are in the cupolas, and on the walls of the right transept. In the cupolas the human figures represent saints but at the same time function as ribs of the structure. On the walls the narrative compositions are spaced with such wide intervals between the different groups, and the figures in the groups are so vertical, that they avoid the aspect of illustrative cartoons on the walls as we find them in the sixteenth-century mosaics in the nave. In the atrium the compositions are more crowded, being copied from early illustrations of the Psalms, but even they avoid horizontal effects and allow the vertical lines to conduct the eye to the caps of the cupolas (plate 18).

In the choir itself the columns of the tabernacle are pre-Byzantine and the Pala d'Oro is not only the most gorgeous and most radiant enamel work, but the most exquisite as illustration, surpassing anything and everything of its own kind in Byzantine art and leaving far behind all other medieval enamel work including Nicholas of Verdun's masterpiece at Klosterneuburg near Vienna.

Except the mural paintings in Yugoslav monasteries and churches, the over-restored but grand mosaics at Daphne near Athens, the copious but inferior ones at Hosios Lucas on the slopes of Helicon and some few at Salonica, Byzantine narrative compositions of before 1300 can be better studied at San Marco than in the whole Aegean world. Even the late fourteenth-century mosaics in the side chapels of San Marco can hold their own with any in the Byzantine world, excepting the earliest mosaics of the decline in the Karieh Djami at Constantinople. By a curious stroke of fortune it is only in Italy that classical Byzantine iconography can be studied and enjoyed to perfection, in San Marco, as we have seen, and even better in Sicily at Monreale and above all in the Cappella Palatina in Palermo.

Nothing of course can take away from the enchantment of seeing where they grew and flourished, no matter how diminished and ruined today. By travelling in Aegean lands and visiting the rare treasures they still contain, one becomes aware of Italy's and Sicily's richness not only in Byzantine art but in classical architecture as well. We only have to recall the temples of Greater Greece in Italy and Sicily, like those of Paestum, Syracuse, Agrigento, Selinunte and Segesta; and mosaics like those of Naples, San Prisco, Rome, Cefalù, Palermo and Monreale.

Similarly, perhaps a thousand years from now, the art of the Western world will have to be sought in the greater Europe of America rather than in the Asiatized Europe of the coming centuries.

Messina,
May 19, 1953

Never since 1889 had I been in a train south of Naples. Had not seen bombed buildings both sides of railway line as one leaves Naples. Man has done here in a minute what it took nature relatively long, for all its violence, in Herculaneum, in Pompeii. Scenery—particularly between Agropoli and Sapri—ever more lush, more semi-tropical, rivalling the Amalfitan coast. Headlands, cliffs, towered heights, ravines, sea-distances. No good beaches. Only narrow strips of iron-grey between land and water. Gigantic olive groves, masses of yellow broom.

Scarcely any foreigners. Heard the nasal voices of an American couple and saw the distinguished face of one elderly Frenchman. Most of the compartments occupied by Italians who seem to be on the move as never before in my sixty years residence in Italy, and travelling comfortably. At Villa San Giovanni an endless Red Cross train with pilgrims to Lourdes. What a tribute to hope!

As the crowded joyous ferry-boat was nearing Messina, I was seized by an ailment perhaps confined to myself and which I have isolated and named. I call it 'Xenodochiophobia'. It makes me sweat with anxiety about what I shall find

44 The Sea-front, Messina (before 1908)

in the hotel that I approach. If the room should be of the wrong shape, too high or too low, too narrow, with furniture out of proportion, dusty, grimy, with torn wallpapers, without a reading lamp by the bed, without a wastepaper basket, I know I shall feel utterly miserable in it. More than once after a long day's motoring and sightseeing in Spain, in Greece, in Syria, in Algeria, have I dreaded so much what awaited me that, tired as I was, I would have preferred to go on and on. My fears with regard to the hotel here at Messina were not groundless. Entrance hall magnificent with double grand staircase leading up to rooms I shall not praise, and the price charged for them is not in proportion to the rooms but to the splendour of the staircase. In compensation (as every where in Sicily) friendly helpful service, wholesome food, swiftly served.

This town is now as vital and bustling as most other provincial capitals of Italy with broad streets and buildings inspired by Exhibition architecture. A certain gaiety prevails, the views on the sea, the sea breeze. Yet I recall nostalgically the Messina that I first visited in 1888 with its noble architectural sea-front, called

Messina,
May 20, 1953

45 Montorsoli: Fountain of Orion (1550), Messina

the 'Palazzata' and parallel with it streets lined with big and small palaces, each of their windows with a balcony caged in with gilded wrought iron. The pavement curving in towards the centre of the street to let the water flow off easily. Few traces of all this remain: the small but exquisite church of the Catalani, Montorsoli's great fountain, perhaps the most wonderful of its kind in Italy, parts of the ancient cathedral, most of which has been heavily and pompously restored.

It is curious that I know of no monograph that reproduces Montorsoli's fountain in all its detail and gives an adequate account of its history. It furnishes a repertorium of Michelangelesque motives the like of which exists nowhere

46 Central porch of Messina Cathedral

except in the work of the great master himself. Apart from its importance in the history of Italian art it is a work of very considerable merit both as a whole, as design and composition, and for its entertaining and at times exquisite detail.

In the northern part of the town, by the sea, the National Museum is now being rearranged in an old monastic building with spacious grounds and cloisters, very suitable for displaying a number of interesting late Antique, medieval, Renaissance and Baroque sculptures and architectural fragments, also mosaics and paintings. Among the last, two famous Caravaggios and several pictures by followers of his. Most of this saved from the various churches and convents destroyed by the earthquake.

Messina,
May 21, 1953

Asked for a morning paper and they brought me one that was so madly anti-De Gasperi and anti-American that I took it for a pro-Soviet sheet. The porter assured me it was the local Monarchist organ. Then he fetched me the *Giornale di Sicilia,* supposed to be *indipendente.* Its tone was scarcely better. What do they want? Do they really prefer Fascists, Communists, Monarchists, anybody who will bring down the present government? Friends here complain of the mistakes De Gasperi has made. Of course he has, but government is an empirical affair, liable to every kind of wrong start and blind alley—indeed too complicated in a parliamentary regime to be carried on by mere human beings, no matter how able. And nobody alive is abler than De Gasperi. The overwhelming majority of Italians when they talk and when they write are far too passionate and lose their heads the moment they begin to discuss politics, treating it not as rational house-keeping but as theology.

Chief reason for our staying three days in Messina is the exhibition of paintings by Antonello da Messina, the one world-renowned painter of Sicily and indeed of the whole of southern Quattrocento Italy. The show contains by no means all his works, none from London or Paris or Washington nor of course his masterpiece, the great 'St Sebastian' of the Dresden Gallery which has, let us hope, only momentarily disappeared. Apparently the Soviet authorities have declared themselves unacquainted with its present whereabouts, but that may be said for diplomatic reasons.[4]

Apart from a number of portraits more than sufficient to give an idea of Antonello's greatness as a portraitist, it contains the 'Annunciation' which Enrico Mauceri[5] discovered at Palazzolo Acreide and the sublime 'Pietà' from the Correr Museum in Venice. Also two 'Crucifixions', an early one from what used to be called Hermannstadt in Transylvania and a maturer one from Antwerp. In both of these and in what remains of the great 'Annunciation' there is in the landscapes a feeling for distance, for (so to speak) lived distance, walked-over distance, that one seldom, perhaps never, gets in the Florentines of

the fifteenth century, despite all their passionate devotion to the study of perspective. Even in the best of them, Piero della Francesca, Baldovinetti, Pollaiuolo, it results in little more than mere topography.

I cannot understand how all of us art critics failed to recognize the mind and
hand of Antonello in the Correr 'Pietà'. Perhaps because it is so overwhelmingly Bellinesque. Nevertheless what remains of landscape and architecture as
well as something in the heads of the angels and in the Byzantine design of their

48 Antonello da Messina: 'Crucifixion' (detail), Sibiù Museum

wings should have given us the clue to the right attribution. All honour to the late Roger Fry for having been the first to find it.

Most mysterious is the career of Antonello. His beginnings as shown in the exhibition are not too promising. The conviction I have had for many years that as a young man he came under the influence of Petrus Christus is now confirmed, as Professor Bottari from Catania tells me, by a document discovered in the Milan archives which speaks of Petrus and Antonello having met and worked together at Milan. In 1474 or '75 he went to Venice, where his altarpiece for San Cassiano created as much excitement as ever a Cézanne in our time has in Paris. For technical reasons no doubt, for as composition it is conventionally Bellinesque and in expression non-committal, dull in fact. He ended by becoming almost entirely a Venetian, as is shown by the 'Pietà', the 'St Sebastian', and the portraits done in the last three years of his life. What he might have grown to if he had not been cut off at the age of forty in February, 1479, leaves one wondering.

49   Antonello da Messina: 'Crucifixion' (1475, detail), Musée Royal, Antwerp

Messina,
May 22, 1953

Among the various visits I made to Sicily, there was one in May 1908. We
drove up to the wooded heights above the town and did so again yesterday,
following the road to Palermo which climbs up swiftly, lined with wonderful
clumps of scarlet-red geraniums, as if through a noble private park, and afford-
ing the most poetical views of sea and sky and headlands. In December of the
same year, 1908, I was at Washington, when one morning the paper brought
in with my breakfast told of the appalling disaster that had overcome this town
the day before. It not only horrified and distressed me for all the victims and the
destruction, but filled me with anguish of anxiety about a dear friend I knew to
be there. He was miraculously saved, but no trace was ever found of his wife
and four children.

Taormina,
May 23, 1953

When I first came to Taormina, the only inn was a small pink house just
under the Greek theatre. How different from the vast caravanserai, inns and
pensions, that now absorb the little town. Little, but with an important role in

the history of ancient Sicily. Like all its sister towns, always at war, even with its village neighbour Mola on a high peak above it. Its crowning glory is the view from the so-called Greek theatre. The curious thing is that when the theatre was, as we Americans say, 'a going concern', the spectators could not have enjoyed what we are seeing now, for like every Greek and Roman theatre it had a permanent architectural scene which precluded any outlook on the landscape. The reconstruction of such a scene at Sabratha and a still complete one at Aspendus in Asia Minor show what a considerable height they reached. I do not recall whether Thucydides actually says that the theatre of Syracuse was crowded with anxious spectators watching the outcome of the battle in the inner harbour in their defence against the Athenians, or if that is a fancy of more recent historians. If Thucydides did say so, then the theatre of Syracuse must have been unlike most, if not all others. I suspect that the ancient Greeks and their docile pupils the Romans did not care for landscapes as views, but only as a feeling for the freshness of morning and evening and as delight in the calm of woodland solitude.

Taormina,
May 24, 1953
Woke at 4.45 this morning and stepped out on the balcony to see the dawn on Etna. Its colour was silver and mauve over a gentle glow from within. A diadem of snow and below a necklace of cloud. The height of the mountain reduced by its soft long slopes. The sea a mirror reflecting and at the same time intensifying the colours of the sky and the sky itself blushing, flushing with the sunlight coming from below and making itself felt, although not yet visible to the eye. A calm with no sound but the muted one of the great expanse of sea breaking as it reached the shore. Wordsworth, in the mood of his sonnet about sunrise on Westminster Bridge, might have been able to communicate to those who had not seen it what the scene meant to me, and the sheer visual happiness, and the sublimity, harmony and solemn silence I enjoyed—so selfishly.

As I have said, the soft slopes of Etna prevent our feeling its great height. But I felt it well enough one morning under the following circumstances. Early in December 1888 I took passage on a tramp steamer at the Piraeus, that was to land me at Messina. The sea misbehaved in the maddest, most boisterous fashion. It calmed down as we were approaching Sicily. I looked up at the crystalline firmament and saw a white curve following it up, it seemed to me almost to the zenith. I asked, what the world it could be? The answer was 'the height of Etna curved with the curve of the sky'. Was it an illusion, was it really so? I have never forgotten the extraordinary vision.

Taormina,
May 25, 1953
What eggs one to leave this so beautiful, so comfortable, so restful place? There is nothing for me to do here, now that I can toddle only with leaden legs and

50 Greek Theatre, Taormina

can no longer take long walks. A prolonged stay after a bit of not unpleasant boredom might lead to my becoming creative again which would procure me greater satisfaction than travelling about from one discomfort to another, to see what I have glorified in my memory from my youthful visits and that now I may find disfigured by every kind of addition and vulgarity. Is it mere *Wanderlust*? I fear for the most part it is. And why do we submit to this universal urge to change place? Why does the tourist kick about from one end of the world to another at such speed? Stopping nowhere, he takes in little besides the recollection that he has been there and that it still is on the map. Has no German yet written on *Reiselust*?

Awoke again at 4.30 and stepped out on the balcony, gazing, seeing, looking, watching the dawn mounting over the Greek theatre and slowly lighting up the sky, the sea and the stretch of country all the way to snow-capped Etna. As I looked at the clustering houses within the hemicycle of its hills, Taormina

Taormina,
May 26, 1953

75

51 Mantegna: 'Agony in the Garden', National Gallery, London

reminded me of something. After an effort to recall it, it turned out to be Mantegna in the National Gallery 'Agony in the Garden', or in the Gardner 'Sacra Conversazione'. Then memory yielded up the fact that I had come to the same conclusion twenty-five or more years ago, when last here. All the while I suffered from a haunting sense of being aphasic, mentally constipated, not knowing how to put into words the impressions I was receiving as I watched first the sunlight and then the sun itself lighting up sombre depths and creeping up the slopes of Etna.

Enna,
May 27, 1953   Although we have not stopped at Catania this time, its name calls up an amusing bit of etymology which can serve as a warning to philosophers too eager to find so-called 'scientific' reasons for the origin of words. In the earlier part of the last century, when lemons were not yet being grown in the USA,

52 General view with the Rocca di Mola, Taormina

American sailing vessels frequently called for them in Sicily and particularly in Catania. The small boys of course gathered round these red-bearded giants from so far away, and when they became too annoying the Americans would yell 'Skedaddle', which in the American language of that time meant 'Get out of the way'. So the common people of Catania ended by calling the Americans 'Gli Schidado', just as the French of the time of Jeanne d'Arc called the English 'Les Godam' and the Tuscan peasants in 1944 called the American soldiers 'Gli Ochei'.

The inflational Verga and the deflational De Roberto both came from Catania, or at least the last one spent his life there even if he came from else-where. Verga, although he treats so much of the peasants and small people, heroizes them. De Roberto, treating of the aristocracy, brings it down to earth. Verga retains his fame and is still read, I hope, not merely in school anthologies. De Roberto seems almost entirely forgotten. One of the most noted of American novelists, the late Edith Wharton, had the greatest admiration for him, and it was she who made me read his masterpiece of a novel *I Viceré*.

54 General view, Centuripe

Last time we were in Catania, twenty-seven years ago, we were taken by Enzo Maganuco to the museum in the Benedictine convent on the outskirts of the town. It contained many objects of interest for an omnivorous art lover like myself. There was one large Antique vase that attracted my special attention and I asked the charming young director what it was. He looked at it for a long time and then said: 'E un vaso'. He turned out to be a recent appointment for journalistic service to the regime and no 'damned merit' by way of preparation for his office.

To come here we have taken a road that circles around Etna, touching Linguaglossa, Randazzo and Bronte, and then at Adrano joins the Catania–Palermo highroad. Again and again we crossed wide rivers of hardened lava wriggling down like snakes from Etna, the recent ones sinister in their unrelieved blackness, the older ones already covered with yellow broom, the flower chosen by Leopardi as symbol of the precarious condition of human life. Almost all the small towns we passed, but particularly Regalbuto and Agira, look at a distance like pyramidal or conical honeycombs, and as you get nearer, the houses seem to be piled like dice, one over the other. Their grouped facets would have rejoiced the eye of a Cézanne more than anything he could find in his own Provence, except perhaps Les Baux.

Getting into and through these towns in a motor is not easy, especially in the late afternoon, when the whole male population seems to be out in the street gesticulating, talking, discussing, and disputing, probably in connection with the approaching elections.

And so to Enna, the most lordly town of all, surpassing for its position even Edinburgh, Toledo, Siena, Perugia, and any other hill town known to me in Europe and in the Mediterranean world. What a place this would be to pass days and weeks in, if only it had a comfortable, clean inn, kept by people who really knew their job and understood that it would be in their and their town's interest to attract foreigners to it.

The situation of the hotel, such as it is, could not be more beautiful. From its windows and from the great terrace-piazza before it one sees the bold profiles of the Castello Lombardo and of the sphinx-like clump of rocks beyond it, and then the whole range of mountains, as far as Etna, which today at dawn I saw in crystalline blue clearness. At night the electric-lit towns, Calascibetta just opposite to us and the others further away, twinkle like fireworks specially arranged for our pleasure. In 1908 I came here in an open car with my wife and my dear friends Carlo Placci and his nephew Lucien Henraux. The hotel was at that time quite tolerable, although of rudimentary comfort. The bill almost took our breath away, the charges being very nearly what they were then in the best hotels at Palermo or Taormina. The hotel-keeper met our protests very readily: 'You slept pretty well, you ate pretty well; how can you expect to get all that up here without paying prices that make it possible for me to keep an inn for travellers like yourselves?'

Enna,
May 28, 1953

No restaurant in this inn, but a well-kept one in the town from where the obliging valet fetched our supper both yesterday and the day before. At lunch-time we went to it ourselves and after two excellent meals were treated as *habitués* and took leave of the owner as of an old friend.

Here, and everywhere in Sicily, both bread and *pasta* are of superlative quality and truly worthy of the reign of Demeter. Perhaps the finest quality of wheat is no longer exported as it used to be.

I must still be grateful to the existence of any kind of inn in this town, for only by spending two nights here have I been able to manage the excursion to the excavations of Casale near Piazza Armerina without too much fatigue. What a landscape to drive through: valleys and hillsides golden with the ripe corn, shaded roads, ash trees, eucalyptus, and the silhouette of Etna rising

80

55　General view of Calascibetta from Enna

above other heights visible from a thirty miles' distance. As we were approach/
ing Piazza Armerina we met more and more cattle and horses and people on
horseback, or rather on mare's back with the colt trotting alongside of them.
In the town we had to bulldoze our way through cattle, horses, pigs, pottery and
every kind of article being marketed. The trappings of the horses and the painted
carts most picturesque, and to match them the riders should have been dressed
like the natives of Arizona or New Mexico, in ponchos and leather stockings.
On the road to Casale, following a signboard with '*Mosaici*' written on it, we
got to a guichet where one pays and is admitted to the excavations. After
heavy rain the path leading down to them was so muddy that we had to borrow
rubber boots from the *custodi* to venture on it.

The site of the villa soon appeared before us marked by scattered remains of
walls and columns showing the vastness of the original buildings. Various sheds

56 Head of a horse,
detail of a mosaic
(fourth century A.D.),
Casale

have been put up recently to roof over the mosaics. In the chief digger and over-
seer of works, Cavaliere Veneziani, we discovered an old friend whom we had
met eighteen years ago as Giacomo Guidi's right hand at Sabratha. He showed
us the more interesting of the semi-polychrome floor mosaics and unpedantically
explained what they were supposed to represent and their probable date.[6] It
clearly was the villa of a very important person. Cavaliere Veneziani suggested
that the owner might have been no less a figure than Maximian, the father of
Maxentius who, setting himself up as the rival of Constantine, was slain in the
epoch-making battle at Ponte Molle. In the great hunting scene the principal
personage, the owner probably of the villa, was undoubtedly meant to be a
portrait and his dress and low round cap are the kind worn in the beginning of
the fourth century. His features do not preclude the possibility—given differ-

ences in technique and quality—of its being the face seen frontally on the gold coins of Maxentius. In the vast composition representing a chase, the most important of the whole lot, we see riders dashing forward and backward, beaters, carts drawn by oxen with cages for wild animals, quantities of tigers, lions, gnus, hippopotamuses, gazelles. The animals done with considerable spirit, the human beings much less so. They are dressed in tight-fitting tunics that reach down to over the knees and anticipate the clothes of ordinary people in the early Middle Ages. Some of them also wear capes with embroidered trimmings. In the centre of the composition, on a river or lake, rowing and sailing boats are kept ready with wooden bridges leading to them from the land, one of which is being crossed by a horseman pursued by a tiger.

Hunting scenes of this type were much in favour at the time when people were used to the cruel gladiatory spectacles in the circus and to a dangerous and violent mode of life. Even the churches, particularly in the peripheral parts of the *oecumene*, were sometimes decorated with such scenes. They furnished amusing and spirited decorations without having to fall back on definitely pagan imagery or to get involved in controversial Christian symbolism. I seem to remember hunting scenes in the early Christian church of Ermita de San Baudelio near Soria in Old Castile.

The principal personage, already referred to as possibly a portrait of Maxentius, stands between two shield-bearers and wears an elaborately embroidered cape reaching down to the ankles. After the triumph of Christianity the fashion of these embroidered capes was taken over by the Church and gradually the floral and geometric designs changed into representations of Gospel stories. They became so extravagant that writers of a generation or two later spoke of people having the whole story of the New Testament on their backs. In a chastened form this kind of cape became the cope—*piviale*—of higher ecclesiastics, which has been worn all through the centuries and is still being used on great ceremonial occasions and in processions. Famous are the copes embroidered all over, like the magnificent one done for Emperor Frederick II in

58 After a design by Botticelli: Embroidered cope (detail), Museo Poldi Pezzoli, Milan

59 Embroidered cope (*c.* 1500),
Perugia University

Palermo and the medieval English ones of which at least two fine examples can
be seen in Italy, one at the Vatican and the other in the small Diocesan Museum
of Pienza near Siena. In the Renaissance the designs for episodes of the Gospel
and stories of saints to be embroidered along the edges and on the back (where
a sort of shield takes the place of the original hood) were frequently furnished

by the best painters of the day. One can also find them represented in pictures, like Fra Angelico's 'Coronation' at the Louvre or Signorelli's great altarpiece in Perugia Cathedral.

Another mosaic, a semi-circular one, has for its subject the fulmination of the Titans, the central figure of which vaguely recalls the upper part of Michelangelo's 'Last Judgment'. The composition must go back to a Hellenistic artist and may originally have had some astrological connotation. Again in a lunette is seated an allegorical figure with a cornucopia in one hand and an elephant's tusk in the other, between elephants and tigers. She reminds me of the city deities that were common in the Hellenistic period, like the colossal third- or fourth-century Roma in the Museo delle Terme.

In some of the mosaics winged putti climb over trellises to pick grapes and call to mind Raphaelesque compositions like Giovanni da Udine's ceilings in the portico of the Villa di Papa Giulio. Most unusual ten female athletes attitudinizing with floral emblems in their hands. They have nothing to wear except a *soutien-gorge* and a *cache-sexe*, a combination of garments re-invented for the young women of recent years who pass their summers basking and baking on the beaches of Cannes and other Riviera resorts.

Interesting both archaeologically and historically as these mosaics certainly are from the point of view of draughtsmanship and quality of line, they are not to be compared with the one great semi-polychrome mosaic that has come down to us, the 'Battle of Alexander and Darius', now in the Naples Museum, done three centuries earlier, nor with the beauty of execution in black and white compositions found so plentifully in central Italy. Above all they recall the mosaics which one finds everywhere in North Africa. I would suggest that they have their origin at Carthage and that the workmen may have come from there. They may go back to inventions of Alexandrian artists, but not as directly as the great mosaic from Palestrina with its display of lotus and papyrus and crocodiles.

Despite the mediocre execution, the Casale mosaics are of high cultural and art-historical interest and it is to be hoped that the excavations will be completed without too much delay.

Looking back at the enclosed valley facing the sun, one realizes that the villa must have offered perfect shelter in the wintry season. And even later, after falling into great disrepair, it yet continued to shelter some inhabitants or some tenants till the Norman period, as is proved by coins found there. Probably the forest, which to the north kept the soil together, was cut down and floods and landslides gradually overwhelmed the whole place, which thus no longer offered shelter to occupants who could have restored it.

It is time to return to our night's quarters at Enna. As we drive back in the sunset light I am pursued by the nostalgic vision of so many country seats and

60 Female athletes, detail of a mosaic (fourth century A.D.), Casale

elegant villas, that must have existed in these and other regions of the classical world from the British Isles to the Sahara Desert, of which no trace is left.

On our way down from Enna we passed through the picturesque fair of Piazza Armerina again and skirted town after town, each climbing from valley to top of hill and crowned by façade and tower of its cathedral. Loftiest of all in position and most elegant in the outlay of streets and Baroque buildings is Palazzolo Acreide, whence came the Antonello 'Annunciation'. At the very top of the town, in a convent-church with a delightfully capricious Rococo facade (plate 42), a noble statue of the Madonna by Francesco Laurana, the mysterious artist, frequently confused with the Dalmatian Laurana, who is supposed to have worked as architect in Urbino. It is, as a matter of fact, hard to put him together, the sculptures attributed to him being of such different character and quality. He seems to have worked chiefly in Provence and southern Italy, producing portraits of women among the most fascinating done in the Renaissance, excepting those of Desiderio only. Yet in compositions ascribed to him in Carcassonne, Marseilles and in Sicilian churches, he is a poor creature. Of the statues of the Madonna all over Sicily ascribed to him, some few are manifestly his while the greater number seem to be by the Gaggini who undoubtedly were under his influence. He deserves more study than hitherto has been devoted to him.

*

What a different Syracuse from the one I knew in 1888! The town was then confined entirely to Ortygia and on the continental side, so to say, there was nothing but the railway station. From this one drove into the old town in broken-down cabs over a castellated bridge, bearing the arms of Charles V. Now a vast modern city has gathered on

61 Francesco Laurana: Eleonora of Aragon, Museo Nazionale, Palermo

62 Francesco Laurana:
Madonna (*c.* 1474),
Chiesa dei
Minori Osservanti,
Palazzolo Acreide

63 Edward Brandard: 'View from Fort Labdalon, Syracuse', engraving

both sides of the narrow water, spanned by a bridge so wide that it appears to be an ordinary street. The quality of insularity is abolished and the sense of compact completeness that went with it.

Unchanged are the water-front, where our so often visited and still highly satisfactory hotel is situated, and the delightful terraces leading up to the papyrus-filled spring of Arethusa (except for its being neon-lit at night), the Arethusa of Shelley's so evocative verses beginning with: 'Arethusa arose—From her couch of snows—In the Acroceraunian mountains.' Nothing more classical than the view, across the great harbour, of Plemyrion and the Iblean hills, yet the head waiter assures us that whoever has been to Lucerne cannot fail to see how identical the view here is to the one there on the lake.

Syracuse,
May 30, 1953
A violent south-wester has prevented our revisiting the classical sites, the theatre, the fort of Euryelus, the Achradina and Epipolae, and the romantic source of Cyane with its papyrus blowing in the breeze and its transparent multi-coloured depth. I have had to confine myself to the two museums and to the Duomo, the former Temple of Athena, roofed over and walled in by a seventh-century bishop. The wonderfully preserved Doric columns of the

64 Spring of Arethusa, Syracuse

65 Fragment of a laver, Museo Medioevale, Palazzo Bellomo, Syracuse

Duomo give one a sense, that one lacks in the fragmentary outdoor ruins, of what a vast space these temples occupied. The medieval museum, placed in an interesting Aragonese palace, is full of Byzantine fragments, among them colonettes that may have come from the Proconnesus in the Sea of Marmara whence they were exported to every part of the Mediterranean world, as far at least as Andalusia where we find them in great numbers in the Khalifian palace of San Jeronimo outside Cordova. The classical museum is most famous for its nude Venus, twin sister almost of the one from Cyrene in the Museo delle Terme, one leaving me as cold as the other. Unusual in quality is a large early Christian

66 Left aisle of the
Cathedral with
columns from the
Temple of Athena,
Syracuse

Early Christian sarcophagus, Museo Archeologico, Syracuse

sarcophagus, not only for the way it treats gospel subjects but for the actual quality of the sculpture. Hall after hall with Attic vases, several of extreme beauty, but wearisome for there being too many of them and because we cannot touch them as well as see them. The museum houses also a world-famous collection of Antique coins, for the making of which Syracuse was supreme. But only the happy few can hope to see them, celebrated archaeologists rather than mere art-lovers like myself.

Syracuse,
May 31, 1953

The waiter in this hotel speaks with regret of the time when travellers stayed, dressed for dinner, took time to enjoy the place. Now they mostly come in huge buses and see the whole of Sicily in six days. 'What do they see?' the old waiter asked. 'They make sure the town they have heard of has not run away.' Travelling, change of place seems to be a physical need, perhaps already of most animals. As for humanity, it seems to have been on the move all the time, if not for other reason than on pilgrimages and even crusades. I recall how as a little boy of six or at utmost seven I longed, yearned to go and see what was beyond the horizon. Moving, going to another town, another village even, used to make me feverish with excitement. And now that I am almost eighty-eight, why am I here, suffering fatigue, discomfort, even boredom, if not of the animal urge 'to make pilgrimage'?

Among the things that, owing to the raging wind I have been prevented from doing here, is to pay my respects to the Palazzo Landolino, still standing, I hope, on the mainland, where a great German poet, Count von Platen, the butt of Heine's most spiteful wit, lived and died in 1835, and lies buried in his host's garden. He was the author of very remarkable sonnets, verses in the Arab mode, and of one of the most nostalgic ballads ever written, that about the burial of Alaric in the Busento at Cosenza.

Sicily has fascinated the Germans even before the Romantic period and before the cult of Frederick and Manfred and the glories of the Hohenstaufen in Sicily and southern Italy. There was the patrician Goethe of course, and a far less known writer, the Hessian sympathizer with the French Revolution, Seume, whose *Spaziergang nach Syrakus* deserves to be translated into English and other languages. It is curious how already these early German writers attempt to tell us what they feel, while the eighteenth-century English gentleman Brydone, in *A Tour through Sicily and Malta*, only tells what he does and what is done to him.

On our way from Syracuse we came through Noto, a fascinating town with its wide streets, sumptuous palaces and churches and grilled balconies. It was planned, as Professor Bottari told me, by the Syracusan architect Rosario Gagliardi after the great earthquake of 1693. Stopped to see the

Vittoria,
June 1, 1953

68 Balconies of the Palazzo Villadorato, Noto

most inspired of all the Laurana Madonnas in the Church of the Crucifixion.

Then Modica and Ragusa, climbing up over deep ravines to heights crowned with magnificent cathedrals; both peculiar in the sense that like early Romanesque churches in Germany their facades rise to a bell-tower. And both were, it appears, built by the same Gagliardi, as are other churches of the same type in this region. Instead of being forbiddingly severe they attract us with their Rococo gaiety. Modica I visited before, in 1908, with Placci and Henraux. Carlo di Rudinì had notified his adherents and they received us with the great-

est cordiality. While waiting for an elaborate dinner to be served, they pressed us into sampling their choicest wines. What with the smoke, the clatter of dishes, the loud talk, and the potent wine, I ended by fainting away and was carried to bed. When I came to myself a few minutes later it was as silent around me as the desert. Not a sound, not a voice. I have often remembered this proof of humanity, of fellow-feeling, the like of which in my experience one does not find to the same degree out of Italy. Nobody is as ready as the Italian to help one in real need, in a need that he can understand and sympathize with.

To our delighted surprise we landed here in a perfectly unpretentious inn with every comfort for the weary traveller. It was not easy to reach it through the compact crowd of males of every age—not one female to be seen—thronging the main street and the piazza. The inn too seemed to be intensely alive with male customers and the owner assured us that to keep good rooms for us had not been easy. We asked whether this was due to the election campaign. Oh no, here we are only interested in the *campagna del pomodoro*—the campaign for tomatoes. Vittoria turns out to be the most important centre in the whole of Sicily for *primizie*, artichokes, peas, beans, tomatoes, grapes, out of season. Buyers come here to choose and negotiate, which explains the surprisingly good hotel. We found the dining-room filled with males, mostly dressed like workmen but manifestly doing themselves very well on food and wine that cannot be inexpensive.

Vittoria's name is not due to battle and victory but to the touching fact that its founder, a Colonna who at the beginning of the seventeenth century acted as viceroy for Spain, named it so out of affection for his daughter Vittoria Colonna. On the central piazza the same kind of Baroque church, but in more modest proportions, as at Modica and Ragusa, and alongside of it a theatre in the classical mode, one of the best in that style to be seen anywhere in Europe. Like most Sicilian towns it has a public garden to put to shame the great cities of the North. We got to its principal entrance ten minutes before twelve and were confronted by a *custode* who rather angrily announced his having to close it at noon precisely. We pleaded our having come from far away to see it and would he not wait until we had been to see the view at the far end of it. No; if this walk took us longer than ten minutes he would close the garden *militarmente* at twelve. So we gave it up, but complained to the inn-keeper. Deeply outraged, he telephoned to the Sindaco who sent an official with excuses and the order to have the garden reopened for us at once. The culprit was there with a bunch of flowers and a very woebegone face, and we made our peace with him. The view at the end of the park over the valley of the Ippari was well worth the quarrel. But how this *custode* reminded me of innumerable experiences in museums when the guards begin to shout and shuffle and clang keys half an hour before closing time and without any possibility of such an amiable *accommodement* as was granted to us in Vittoria.

Agrigento,
June 2, 1953
Meanwhile we have reached Agrigento, driving through rich agricultural stretches of land, the immense fields of ripe golden corn separated from the sea by a narrow strip of beach, while the headlands of Gela and Licata rise up so sharply that one wonders whether this coast may not have been very different in 800 B.C. from what it is now. The sea must have crept much farther inland,

isolating the towns and making them far more defensible and at the same time
more independent and more hostile to one another. How I wish I knew enough
geology to substantiate what I suspect. My wife used to complain about our not
being able to afford carrying along a geologist and a botanist on our travels to
tell us exactly what the land was like in past ages and what grew upon it. The
whole of Sicily must have been surrounded by rocky islets which now are like
knobs projecting from an oval dish. As for the trees and flowers, I recall
nostalgically the pleasure I had in Greece in 1888 in the company of my fellow

72 John Cousen: 'Temple Area, Agrigento, from the South', engraving

traveller, a Dutch biologist and botanist who later became the head of the world-famous botanical gardens at Buitenzorg in Java. He could tell me what grew in ancient times on Greek soil and what had been added since. A privilege such as in days gone by only princes would enjoy when on one of their tours of instruction. As we came in sight of the temples of Acragas, the sun was setting, transfiguring the columns of these simple but most harmoniously proportioned

73 Arthur Willmore: 'Temple of Concord, Agrigento', engraving

74 Limoges casket in the sacristy of Agrigento Cathedral (twelfth century)

structures, as if they had been lit from within. Nowhere in Greece, excepting the Parthenon, do we get such an evocation of Hellenism.

Yesterday we had one of the few really perfect days granted to us since we started on our tour. Spent the morning in the town itself, looking at the admirable Limoges twelfth-century caskets in the sacristy of the Duomo and at the

Agrigento,
June 3, 1953

75, 76 Two heads of giants from the Temple of Zeus, Agrigento Museum

famous Phaedra sarcophagus so much admired by Goethe. It is poor in execution but excellent as composition. As we were passing through the sacristy we
glanced at its walls covered with dust-bitten portraits of its former dignitaries.
Who now looks at them, who knows their names, who cares who they were
and what they achieved!

In the museum some good Attic vases and impressive colossal heads from the
Temple of Zeus, also some fine Roman Republican portraits.

The old quiet Girgenti of my first visit in 1888 is now a hustling market-town
with a crowded piazza and a post-office in the Babylonian style introduced by
the Fascist imperial architects.

Returned to the temples in the afternoon, pacing from one to the other,
enjoying the light and wondering what the great town looked like, rising to
what are now the cathedral and the Rupe Atenea. The huge telamon from the
Temple of Zeus, lying on the ground, vies in size with the colossi of Egypt.
Perhaps it was direct Egyptian influence that made the Greeks of southern
Sicily so close to Africa in their attempts to build and to sculpt in a mode
utterly out of touch with human proportions. Even Athens did not entirely

77　Sarcophagus of Phaedra in the sacristy of Agrigento Cathedral (third century B.C.)

escape the ambition of doing the colossal, but no Hellenic town tried it again after the fifth century. The Temple of Concord remains relatively so intact because it was turned early into a Christian church and its closest surroundings into a cemetery. There must have been prodigiously massive high walls all along the escarpment of the temple zone, for in the huge masses hurled down by earthquake there are evidences of many graves which must have been dug out of the walls. This makes it seem likely that the temples themselves were not visible, as they are now, from the sea, all the more so because the sea must have been much nearer to them. I seem to have read somewhere that the columns of

the temple were originally stuccoed. Could they have been more beautiful then than they are now, so warm and honey coloured? It makes me nostalgic for the old days when I had the leisure to spend hours sitting there, leaning against one of the columns, smelling the thyme and reading Theocritus and Virgil.

Sixty-five years ago, on a mild late autumn night, my travelling companion and myself started on foot to see the temples lit by the full moon. We had got half-way when we became aware of the tramp of horses behind us. Two carabinieri rode up and invited us very courteously to turn back for reasons that seemed convincing enough to make us give up our romantic dream.

Castelvetrano, June 5, 1953

Yesterday between Agrigento and Selinunte we stopped in the charming coast town, Sciacca, to look at churches and palaces and fifteenth-century sculptures, including another Madonna attributed to Laurana. Reached Selinunte in time to enjoy it thoroughly in the later afternoon light, picking our way among these piles of colossal capitals and drums of columns lying as they were tumbled down by earthquakes. Selinus, even more than Acragas, attempted the colossal on the Egyptian scale and one wonders where a town on the outskirts of the Greek world could find the labour for such gigantic structures. To build the Parthenon and the Propylaea, Athens could squeeze contributions from its reluctant allies. Here, there were only the great cornfields, supplemented with oil and wine crops. The Fascist regime is *benemerito* for having had part of the columns of the great temple on the acropolis re-erected, and for having extended the road, making it possible for the traveller to drive up to it. It tends, however, to make one concentrate one's attention on this site and to neglect the impressive ruins further inland. It would take a gifted prose-writer to give an idea of this place, to describe the emotions and evocations that it

80 Francesco Laurana: Madonna, Sciacca

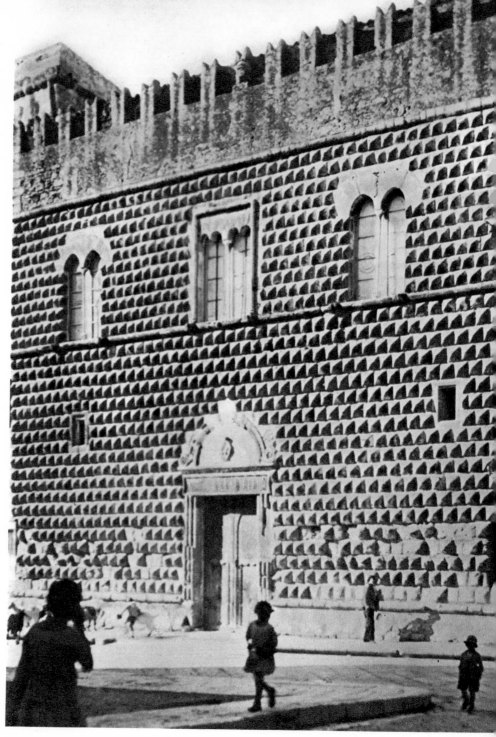

1 Palazzo 'Lo Steripinto',
   Sciacca

arouses in the spectator. Perhaps only a great elegiac poet like Leopardi, or Shelley, or Keats could communicate it to the gentle reader.

This inn, or better night-shelter, has not improved with the years and the vicissitudes of the last war. But I must again be grateful for it, as it would have tired me too much to reach another centre after the visit of Selinunte. All the heavy work, the carrying of luggage seems to be done by a boy of thirteen. Able, quick, intelligent, he could go far if he had a chance. Here he works for his mere keep.

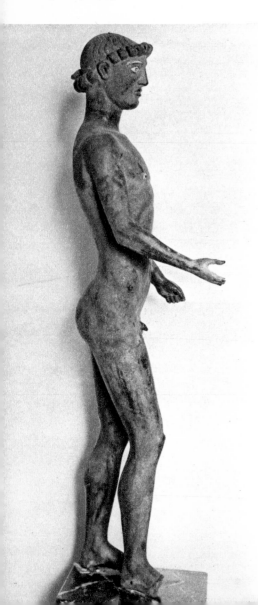

Castelvetrano seen in daylight appeared to us disgustingly dirty; refuse and dust and ragged papers whirled along the streets by the wind and into one's eyes. As we tried to get access to the *Municipio* in order to see the early bronze Kouros from Selinunte, we found it invaded by black-gowned furies of women, screaming, gesticulating, protesting. We were told by the official who led us to the room where the Kouros is kept that the town government was on strike and that no work done for it had been paid in four months.

In contrast Mazzara del Vallo seemed particularly attractive, well-kept, with a beautiful cathedral close and a fine public garden on the sea-front. In the cathedral several Antique sarcophagi, one particularly striking of proto-Ravennate, perhaps Constantinopolitan workmanship, representing Meleager and the Calydonian boar.

Lunch and rest at Marsala in a well-kept inn. In the cathedral fine columns of various African marbles and great preparations going on for the Corpus Christi procession, little girls peacocking in their bridal first communion finery.

On to Erice by a hairpinny road with views of the sea and headlands getting ever finer and more extensive. On the top, towering over pine groves, the elegant little town with its romantic castle and the entirely French cathedral porch, while the inside is of the purest Louis-Philippe Gothic. We are told that the late Victor Emmanuel III came here frequently to enjoy peace and solitude far from the madding crowd.

82 Kouros from Selinunte, Municipio, Castelvetrano

83 Castello, Erice

84 Roman sarcophagus with 'Meleager hunting the Calydonian Boar' (second century A.D), Mazzara del Vallo Cathedral

The old part of Trapani is laid out in the typical Roman fashion with narrow lanes crossing at right angles, all packed full of people dashing forward and backward. Many palaces, some with succulently florid Aragonese portals, the rest Baroque. On the whole a lordly town with fine public gardens. We walked about in the streets and, as there seemed to be an unusual number of opticians' shops, we entered the most elegant looking and asked if a pair of spectacles too wide for me could be fitted into a new frame. They had nothing to suit me. We asked the same question in a much more humble-looking shop and without hesitating a moment the optician bent my spectacles over a small electric heater to the shape that suited me perfectly. It reminded me of the story told me by a German friend of how in the Polish Corridor a tourist car broke down in a small village and nobody seemed to be able to discover why the motor would not work any longer. Finally a Jewish migrant mechanic was sent for and he, after giving the car a few knocks with a small hammer, made it work again. He asked for thirty zlotys, which seemed very excessive to the tourists. 'You only gave a few knocks with your hammer!' 'Ten zlotys for having come and twenty *für gewusst wohin*—for having known *where* to knock.' But my Trapani optician friend would not accept any payment for having known *how* to bend my spectacles.

This very decent inn is looked after in every detail by the owners themselves who could not be more courteous and helpful. Again many of the customers of the restaurant seem to be dressed like workmen and one wonders how they can

85 John Cousen:
'Distant View of the
Temple, Segesta', engraving

86 Temple with Monte Varvaro, Segesta

afford it, unless they have special *accommodements*. Or has it become the fashion to look as if you belonged to the working class even if you don't? It seems a pity to create an artificial class distinction in a country like Italy where the physical type is almost identical at all social levels.

Wonderful drive to Segesta yesterday afternoon. First glimpses of the temple from the high road most romantic, but too small to affect the landscape as it does when near at hand. It is on the whole as impressive as ever, an affirmation of reason, order, intelligence in the midst of the pell-mell, the indifference, the anarchy of nature. The columns are not to be compared with those of Paestum, or the Parthenon, or Bassae, for they lack the elegant swelling in the middle and seem to have been pressed down in a mould widening from capital to base. Is it possible that they have been left unfinished? I seem to remember an archae-ologist friend telling me that the last refinements were done on the spot. Unfor-tunately I was unable to manage the walk to the theatre on the site of the ancient

87, 88 School of Nino Pisano: Madonna, with and without ex-votos, Santuario dell'Annunziata, Trapani

Egesta, or Segesta as the Romans preferred to call it. Egesta did not sound agreeable to their ears, being too much like the Latin word for indigence. Why should a city have grown up in this situation? Perhaps because it was so defensible.

The din and the clatter of the election campaign went on with increasing vehemence until past midnight. It had in a mild way something of the uncontrollable carnival spirit of an American presidential election and might be considered as a quinquennial *sfogo*. If I did not know what it was all about, it would have been just as unintelligible to me as was the cackle of hundreds and thousands of geese in Lithuania, where I spent my childhood. I remember trying to get as near to them as possible in the hope of making out what they were saying.

Palermo,
June 7, 1953

Yesterday forenoon at Trapani we went first to the Santuario della Santissima Annunziata where the famous cult-image—a Madonna of the school of Nino Pisano—is no longer completely encased in gold and silver watches and jewels and trinkets as I saw it in 1908. In the adjoining former convent, with grand cloisters and staircases and vast corridors reminding one of Sankt Florian in Austria, the Museo Pepoli is housed. In 1908 its creator, Count Pepoli, was still alive and did the honours to us. I recall his showing us the guillotine and

89 Baroque staircase in the former Convent of the Annunziata (Museo Pepoli), Trapani

explaining with a certain pedantic satisfaction how it worked. The museum contains a variety of church and lay furniture, some Antique objects, an indif/ ferent collection of late paintings and, best of all, a fine show of ceramics.

Reached Palermo in the late afternoon after another delightful drive on excel/ lent roads, another glimpse of the solitary temple of Segesta, a rather sordid impression of Partinico, ending up with wonderful coast scenery.

This hotel, Villa Igea, has the grandest and most numerous salons I have ever seen, reading and writing rooms, bars, on different levels, with a huge garden filled with palms and every kind of sub/tropical plant, all right on the sea, and across the gulf the jagged skyline of the mountains. It gives one the curious sensation of being on a super/Atlantic liner, gliding so smoothly that you do not feel the motion. All in good order and good taste, regardless of expense. It can house, I am told, 180 guests. At present there are about eighteen. How can it pay? It belongs to a time before the first world war when to the average person

90 Mosaic in Roger's Apartment, Palazzo Reale, Palermo

nothing seemed to mar the horizon of our increasing well-being and our freedom to enjoy living in the beauty and comfort of an hotel of this type.

Palermo,
June 9, 1953

Spent yesterday morning in the Cappella Palatina, a jewel of Byzantine art, with a gorgeous, almost purely Arab honeycomb ceiling. Quality of the mosaics not of the best, drawing parallel to Deodato Orlandi, the thirteenth-century Luccese painter. In the former Palazzo Reale, Roger's apartment with its magnificently conventionalized trees and beasts, a perfect composition, more Persian or at most more Seljuk than Arab. The palace unfortunately not as well kept as it should be but repairs and restorations are being planned.

Palermo,
June 10, 1953

Returned to Monreale. The delight the church gives me is almost spoilt by my despair over not being able to make it, the whole and the details, my own, like a possession I always could lay hold of at need, to enjoy again, in spite of garish and sometimes even uncouth restorations. The effect of the whole is so gorgeous,

91 Oriental ceiling, Cappella Palatina, Palermo

so super-terrestrial, that its medieval congregation could not help feeling it like a forecourt of heaven, like Jerusalem the golden of the hymnal. And what a complete illustration to the narrative parts of Holy Writ and the lives of saints. In the cloister variety of capitals—*each different from the other*, as the guide invariably proclaims—some of exquisite quality as composition, interpretation and carving. The best of them are Burgundian and remind me of those seen at Nazareth in Palestine in the small museum near the Church of the Annunci-

92 Interior of Monreale Cathedral

93 Capitals with the 'Annunciation', Cloister of the Benedictines, Monreale

ation. Knowing, as we now do, that any number of architects, sculptors, and even fresco painters, were among the crusaders, it does not seem at all unlikely that single sculptors, or perhaps groups of them, should have stopped over in Sicily on their way to the East and that traces of the same type of work are found here and there.

In the Museum of Antique Art I was struck again by the uniformity of 'style' in every part of the Greek world and its cultural dependencies, as for instance

Palermo, June 11, 1953

94 Capitals with William II offering the urch to the Madonna', Cloister of the Benedictines, Monreale

95 'The Rape of Europa',
metope from Selinunte,
Museo Nazionale, Palermo

Etruria. A uniformity even greater than that of the art of today radiating from
Paris. All frontal or in profile. The interest of the Archaic artist was concentrated on form so that movement is comparatively neglected. The latest metopes
from Selinunte have attained perfection of form, but the action, the movement
is still awkward and limited. This tends to confirm the thesis that the tactile
values were the first objective of Archaic masters in Greece as among all gifted
primitives. A fairly large Etruscan collection in this museum proves how little
there is in Etruscan art that was not taken from the Greek. Etruscan art represents a slight variant in subject matters and in inferiority of execution. Only

through the originality of incompetence can it be distinguished from the art of the Greeks.

As the Tempio of Rimini encases a Gothic interior with a Renaissance exterior, so the cathedral of Palermo encases a seventeenth-century interior with a medieval exterior. It is inconceivable to me that such a superb building in the capital of the Norman-Swabian empire could have been left undecorated. There must have been mosaics there, as important and as beautiful as those of Monreale. I recall reading somewhere that the seventeenth century destroyed them

Palermo,
June 12, 1953

97 'The Triumph of Death' (detail), fresco, Palazzo Abbatelli, Palermo

with an indifference or even an hostility towards the art of the past that characterizes all epochs convinced of the infinite superiority of their own. Sometimes the architects limited themselves to covering them over with whitewash. At Messina for instance several important mosaics were discovered in the apse of the cathedral during the restoration after the earthquake of 1908.

The tombs of the Normans and Hohenstaufen royalties must have been modelled on the imperial ones at Constantinople in the Church of the Apostles, now the Fatimieh Mosque.

Returned to the charming Oratory of San Lorenzo where Serpotta anticipates the Directoire and even the Empire style, and to San Francesco to see the interesting architectural details brought out by the bombardment and subsequent excellent restoration. At the *Municipio* the Catalan 'Triumph of Death', formerly in the Palazzo Sclafani, much more dramatic than the Pisan one.[7] Some heads foreshortened in a way no mid-fifteenth-century Italian would have attempted.

98 Porphyry socle on the Tomb of Frederick II, Palermo Cathedral ▶

99 Decorative sculptures, Villa Palagonia, Bagheria

<table>
<tr><td>Palermo,
June 13, 1953</td><td>Been to Villa Valguarnera at Bagheria and looked at one of the finest views from its vast garden terrace. And then to Palagonia with its grotesque statues and beautiful carving of every bit of stone. All sordid, breaking up, carried away. The pity of it! Millions are being spent on restoring third-rate paintings and frescoes that might be used to save monuments of taste and craftsmanship of the fascinating eighteenth century. Their disappearance all over Italy—and, alas, over England and Central Europe as well!—will obliterate great chapters of art history.</td></tr>
<tr><td>Palermo,
June 14, 1953</td><td>Returned to the Zisa, a double cube or rather one cube piled on another. It gives one a sense of power, order, elegance, as perhaps no other surviving</td></tr>
</table>

100 Chapel of the Villa Palagonia, Bagheria

medieval building, but shorn of all its splendour and its capacity for giving pleasure by the squalor of its surroundings. Restorations are being planned for the palace and the garden but the houses all around will remain unchanged I fear.

The old Palermo that I first saw in 1888 stopped at the Opera House which was not yet completed. The residential quarter, now almost as extensive as the old town itself, one scarcely dreamt of. The old town has lost much of its splendour. The aristocratic magnificence of its two principal thoroughfares meeting at the Quattro Canti and the fine equipages pacing leisurely are gone. The streets are too noisy and overcrowded to be enjoyable, nobody seems to be out for the pure pleasure of being out, everybody hurried and fussed. The bombardments have played havoc with the palaces that rose right on the sea. Now an esplanade, convenient no doubt, but ugly, spreads between them and the water's edge. Palaces further inland also have been damaged by bombs or have

102　John Cousen:
'View of Old Palermo',
engraving

103　Edward Brandard:
'The Old Promenade,
Palermo', engraving

come down a good deal, but the representatives of the oldest families still manage to live their distinguished almost eighteenth-century life of cultured leisure. Despite this impression made on a *revenant* after sixty years or more, I feel that the change is superficial. All classes of the people seem still ready to join in the periodical outbursts of enthusiasm over political or religious events. Santa Rosalia is still omnipresent and I have no doubt that had I had the luck to participate in her feast, I should have found Goethe's account of it quite adequate.

Mentioning Goethe yesterday made me turn to his immortal descriptions of Sicily. What impresses me most this time is his getting so absorbed in the gesta-tion of his writing that it makes him forget the discomforts he is suffering. On the way from Naples to Palermo by sea he feels seasick, lies relaxed flat on his back, taking nothing but red wine and bread, and ignoring nausea manages to turn his thoughts to the completion and perfecting of his *Tasso*. As he wanders about Palermo and looks and takes in, he keeps thinking about his work and about a *Nausikaa* he thought of writing. His method is not to take notes but to think out a theme completely before he writes it down. With a touch of almost boyish complacency he says that he can easily fill in all the detail from his own experiences of encounters and partings, not so tragic as between Nausicaa and Ulysses, yet nostalgic enough.

Sitting down in a public garden, irresistible curiosity gets hold of him about the plants in which he hopes to discover the *Urpflanze*—the first growth—out of which all others sprang. As a sightseer he is blind to the Middle Ages. No mention of the Norman and Swabian achievements so dear to the Germans of the Romantic period. No visit recorded to their tombs in the cathedral. He speaks of riding through Monreale but does not seem to have looked at the mosaics nor at the matchless carvings in the cloisters, just as some months before passing through Assisi he made no reference to San Francesco and all its marvellous Trecento paintings. Such a genius and yet so limited in his visual tastes, he expresses and interprets only the admirations that were current in his epoch and accepted in the cultural world he belonged to before coming to Italy. If, in following his steps I notice his indifference to what is our chief delight now, I do not by any means want to belittle the importance of his pages. I want only to point out the distance created by different cultural traditions between us and eminent men of other ages.

He appreciates the sumptuousness of his lodgings in what in my time has been the splendid Palazzo Butera right on the sea. As there were no classical remains to be examined at Palermo, he abandons himself to the enjoyment of the scenery and is fascinated by the cynical good humour of its inhabitants, by the

104 Entrance to the Grotto of St Rosalia, Monte Pellegrino, Palermo

whimsical absurdities of people in high places. Describes the unspeakable
filthiness of the streets and how it was accepted as unavoidable.

Remembering that Palermo was the birthplace of Cagliostro, the eighteenth-
century mage, miracle worker and impostor who would have put to blush the
most famous spiritualistic humbugs and *swamis* of our day, Goethe looks up his
family, with a certain bad conscience about the fibs he has to tell in order to
approach them. He speaks with touching sympathy of their humble but dignified way of living and the noble resignation of Cagliostro's old mother.

Goethe goes to Bagheria and is shocked and outraged by the sculptured
monsters and grotesques of the Palagonia, because, as usual in his enjoyment of
visual art, he sees only the shapes and very seldom the quality of the execution.
A few days later he encounters in the street a distinguished elderly gentleman in
court dress followed by liveried servants holding out dishes for alms. On
inquiry he finds that it is the creator and owner of the Palagonia who is collect-
ing what sums he may gather for freeing Christian slaves in North Africa. And
Goethe's heart softens towards him, although he wishes that instead of wasting
his money on follies he had given it all up on such noble purposes. Riding
through the centre of the island, he encounters more and more miserable
lodgings, with the exception of Alcamo, and speaks of Enna or Castro-
giovanni—*toute proportion gardée*—as I have recently done, that is to say, not

View of Palermo with the Cathedral and Monte Pellegrino

drawing a veil over the material discomforts suffered in a place that should be a paradise.

His great preoccupation everywhere, not only in the country but even in the towns, is mineralogical, not so much for the stones themselves as for what they tell him about the geological formation. At Girgenti he is at his happiest, in raptures over the temples that we still enjoy so much and over many picturesque ruins between them and the acropolis that have since disappeared.

Accompanied by a draughtsman—how happy an up-to-date Kodak would have made him!—and wandering with him through landscapes that seem sublime to us as distance and skyline, he complains of there being nothing to inspire the pencil of his friend. Only the fore-edge existed for them.

Not only the Sicilian, but the whole of his Italian journey demonstrates how time-bound even a genius like Goethe could not avoid being. We think in vain that we are free to look and see and appreciate everything on earth. Even the most gifted of us can never get much beyond what he was taught to understand during his formative years.

Palermo,
June 16, 1953

Our last day. Went up to Monte Pellegrino on a glorious morning and was sad at having to leave all this matchless beauty. If only one could possess it all and keep it, one would be a god.

106 Head of Neptune,
mosaic, Tripoli Museum

Many of my friends, being by now thoroughly air-minded, are indignant with me for taking this journey to Tripoli by such old-fashioned methods of loco-motion as train and ship. Just now I feel as if they may be right for I have not found the famous *Freccia del Sud* quite as agreeable as I expected. It shakes one up badly by obliging one to push and stumble twice through the crowded, draughty corridors of six or seven carriages in order to reach the dining-car and fight one's way back from there. Besides, from Rome on it might be more appropriately called *Freccia del Digiuno*. A rather late breakfast may be obtained on the ferry-boat and a *cestino* at the station of Catania but otherwise nothing is provided for the sustenance of the traveller.

Nevertheless I am delighted to be here in perfect weather and glorious light and to see again what two years ago I was prevented by a raging *libeccio* from revisiting. First of all the Greek theatre, wonderful geometrically but spoilt by factory chimneys and suburban buildings that have grown up between it and the sea. Then the fort of Euryelus which happily remains one of the most impressive sights of Antiquity. No sordid houses anywhere to be seen and the silence of a world where for centuries nothing has happened.

Contrary to the *Freccia del Sud* this boat of the Tirrenia line is a pleasant sur-prise. It had been described to me as old and run down and I find it clean and well looked after, with sufficient space for walking about, attentive service and a charming captain. Among the passengers an old friend, Giacomo Caputo, with whom twenty years ago, when he was a young inspector of the monuments at Bengasi, we spent several days at Cyrene. After Guidi's death he became Superintendent in Libya and directed the excavation of the theatre at Leptis. He is now returning to Leptis to take last notes and measurements before pub-lishing this important discovery.

I was whisked away by my hostess yesterday morning from the quay and left my companions to deal with customs formalities. Heard later that it had not been easy to secure porters because of Ramadan being in full progress, the great Muslim fast when no food or drink may be touched from sunrise to sunset. Who can blame the porters for shirking their work under such circumstances?

On driving through the town to this secluded house on the outskirts, I noticed little change. The Lungomare still magnificent, one of the finest sea-fronts in the whole Mediterranean, the public gardens well kept up, the white-washed houses looking clean. This villa, once the property of the Karamanlis, was bought by Giuseppe Volpi about twenty-five years ago and now belongs to his daughter, our hostess. In spite of all the *conforti moderni* it provides, the mysterious charm of an oriental dwelling has not been spoilt. It is as if the house

107 Patio, Saniet Volpi,
Tripoli

turned its back on the street, from which only a bare white wall pierced by two
massive green *portoni* is visible, and as if it only wanted to watch in gentle
contemplation over its inner life. From the central patio, supported by elegant
marble columns and with a murmuring fountain in the middle, the cool
pleasant living-rooms and other small courts and passages are reached, and
through these last the oasis-garden where the stems of the palms rise up like the
columns of an ideal mosque over a carpet of flowers planted in regular squares
and cut by small channels for irrigation. A blaze of colour on the ground, on

108 Oasis-garden,
Saniet Volpi, Tripoli

the flowering trees and shrubs, on the walls covered with bougainvillia, and a fascinating play of light and shade as the breeze gently moves the branches of the palms.

Tripoli,
May 7, 1955

I feel about as lazy and slack as the observers of the Ramadan fast and not up to any exertion. Walking about in the garden, sitting by the pond with the water-lilies, reading or being read to, chatting, dreaming, watching the sunset from the roof terrace satisfies me completely My hostess has invited the Superintendent of Monuments, Ernesto Vergara Caffarelli, for me, a highly intelligent, active and well-trained archaeologist and an attractive human being. It is to the credit of the Libyan government to have appointed another Italian, when Caputo (who had kept his position during the war and the difficult after-war years with great tact) was appointed Superintendent of Antiquities for the whole of Etruria. Vergara seems to get on well with the officials he depends from and manages to do an astonishing amount of work in spite of receiving very meagre financial help.

Tripoli,
May 11, 1955

With Vergara to Sabratha where Guidi took us twenty years ago, and delighted to find that the avenue leading to the excavations now bears Guidi's name. Unfortunately too tired to take the whole round of the ruins but able to enjoy the fine mosaics and portrait busts in the museum and the reconstruction of the theatre which had been barely begun twenty years ago. The olive plantations

109 Theatre, Sabratha

110 Great floor mosa
Sabratha

along the road have developed magnificently and a number of concessions seem still to be in Italian hands. Others look abandoned. How much human industry and perseverance and capital has been expended here during the Italian occupation. One cannot help wondering what will happen once the Allied control comes to an end. Will the Libyans want to carry on and preserve what may seem to them an intrusion from a hostile world? And even if they are by now wise enough to understand the immense value of all this improvement, will their Lords and Masters the Senussi allow them to preserve it? It appears that there is no love lost between the two regions. The Libyans consider themselves, and I believe quite rightly so, more urbanized and have no very high opinion of their nomadic masters But I hear too little of what goes on politically in this haven of peace and tranquillity and cannot presume to form any judgment.

Leptis Magna,
May 15, 1955

I am deeply touched by all the trouble taken to make this excursion possible for me. Vergara has put the rooms at the back of the museum at our disposal, Caputo and his assistant who were living in them have gone away to let us have them, my hostess has organized a minor house-move to make us all and particularly me absolutely comfortable for two days. And most miraculous of all, a kind of push-cart on four wheels that can be rolled on the Décauville rails and that used to serve visiting *gerarchi* and notables is ready for me and spares me the

112 Forum of Septimius Severus, Leptis Magna

113 Basilica of Septimius Severus, Leptis Magna

trudge through the vast expanse of the ruins. Four labourers push and pull me from one site to the other, while Vergara is there to explain and elucidate.

My most vivid impression of twenty years ago, the great basilica, is more than confirmed by what I see now. In every detail there is an elegance free from any Baroque over-floridness as, for instance, at Baalbek. The great sculptured pillars are so delicately undercut that the effect is almost of lace work, reminding one of the best Indian sculpture or the façade of Mschatta in Moab (most of which is in the Berlin Museum), or of Carolingian ivories of the same date.

Leptis Magna,
May 16, 1955

The most fascinating part of this visit is the theatre dug up under the direction of Caputo since we were here in 1935. By far the best preserved stage, orchestra and seats, and sufficient remains of the top colonnade to let one imagine the whole complete. Another feature I do not remember seeing anywhere else, at least not so clearly recognizable, is a colonnaded ambulatory, originally roofed over (corresponding to what would nowadays be called a 'foyer') built in a semi-circle around the remains of a temple.

I am no longer as I used to be, consumed with curiosity and eagerness to reconstruct ruins into their original shape. Partly, no doubt, because I can no longer run about like a puppy snuffling at every stock and stone. But I always have enjoyed ruins romantically, if the surroundings admitted it, if they were not in the midst of crowded towns like the Rotonda now included in the grounds

114 Decorative tendril from a pilaster, Basilica of Septimius Severus, Leptis Magna

115 Theatre, Leptis Magna

of the Central Station in Rome. And I still love to muse and dream and visualize ruins as a scene, as romance, as a transporting evocation.

Leptis is, all considered, one of the most impressive fields of ruins on the shores of the Mediterranean and can stand the comparison even with Palmyra, the desert port, and with Baalbek, its gigantic columns and its over-blown floreated decoration. There is still much to be excavated in Leptis. The port, for instance, appears to be intact under layers of hardened mud and would be fascinating to reconstitute. Further work will depend on what all of us who love our classical past will be willing to contribute.

In a horse-cab through the whole length of the town to the quadrifrontal Arch of Marcus Aurelius. Had forgotten how complete the stone cupola is and how dignified and noble the figures of prisoners in the remaining but fast disintegrating reliefs. From there we wander through the oldest quarter of the town. Neither in the souks of Cairo or of Aleppo or of Damascus have I had such an impression of exotic Orient and remoteness from the West as in the souk here.

Tripoli,
May 19, 1955

Picturesque and paintable in the style of Delacroix and Decamps and all the other Orientalizing artists. How wise of the Italians, when they built the new Tripoli, to have left the Oriental town almost intact. No thought as in Florence of removing the *antico squallore* and replacing it with the *vita moderna*. Yet the souks must be airless, suffocating and filthy, making Westerners itch to aerate and clean them. The Arab takes these conditions as natural and unquestionable. He gives them his unconscious approval and would miss them if they were changed.

Tripoli,
May 21, 1955   New moon, which means that the great fast should be over and a tripudium of feasting and rejoicing set in. But no, they tell us that calculations such as we believe in are of no avail and that if the new moon has not been seen by those appointed to watch out for it, the fast cannot be called off. Friends who know the Near Eastern countries pretty thoroughly tell us that in none of them have they found, as one does here, meticulous observance of the fast by almost one

hundred per cent of the Muslim population. For four weeks work that can be put off like that of artisans, masons, carpenters almost comes to a standstill while unavoidable work is carried on in an atmosphere of nervous tension and quarrelsomeness. It is surprising that the laxity in observing the rules of the Koran prevalent in Egypt should apparently find no imitators here, seeing that whatever comes from Cairo, papers, radio, cinema and even the time (one hour in advance of Prague), is worshipped here.

Tripoli,
May 22, 1955

The new moon has been seen and the sounds of drums and fifes and general rejoicing reach even our retreat. In driving to the museum of the Castello I was amused to see the life in the streets so changed, so much gayer and livelier. Everywhere are seen groups of picturesque figures in clean white togas and new mightily creaking shoes, and cartfuls of men of all ages are driven out to some festive meeting. It seems that there is an elaborate protocol for wishes to be exchanged when friends meet again after the great fast, safely delivered from a public calamity.

Taken over the Castello by Vergara, a remarkable palimpsest of earlier and later buildings, a labyrinth of passages, stairs, terraces, quiet inner courts with ample room for the various collections, prehistoric, ethnological, classical, Arabo-Turkish, all very well displayed (plate 106). In the basement, and still waiting for their proper place, a group of late Antique reliefs found in the 'hinterland', fascinating examples of the disintegration of form. As *bonne bouche* Vergara shows me a recently found and very puzzling small ivory representing

117 Relief from Ghirza (sixth century A.D.), Tripoli Museum

118, 119 Crouching figure in ivory, probably Alexandrine (second century A.D.), Tripoli Museum

a crouching figure in a ritual position with legs crossed and right arm across his chest. Exquisitely worked. Must be a sacred object and suggests the possibility of having been done in Alexandria *circa* A.D. 200 for a Hindu merchant. It reminded me of Herman Melville's description of the South Pacific Queequeg in an ecstasy of prayer.

Tripoli,
May 24, 1955

Lovely drive to the Oasis of Tagiura with its grand, austerely simple mosque, one of the oldest, I believe, in this region. The forest of Antique columns reminds one of the cathedral of Cordova and the mosques of Damascus and Kairouan. Outside, in the village and in the palm groves, such remoteness from the West and at the same time closeness to Antiquity. Often I have wondered how a Roman wore his toga. Here rich and poor wear it, be it dazzling white or dirty greyish, new or in rags, and stride along utterly unaware of how Antique they look to us. Old men recline on stone benches waiting for the hour of the evening prayer, as distinguished and impressive as the figures in Bellini's Naples 'Transfiguration'.

On board the
Argentina,
May 26, 1955

Back on our boat, received with the greatest cordiality and excellently cared for. Weather less favourable than on our outward voyage. A baby *ghibli* is trying to gather strength and makes the air oppressive and the sky glaring and leaden. But it is interesting to get the view of town and sea-front in this strange, somewhat sinister light, typical for the Mediterranean countries. Looking back on the three weeks spent in Tripoli I feel very grateful for a real rest cure in a world remote and secluded enough to create a sense of complete detachment from one's usual routine of work and duties and worries.

120   San Marco, Rossano Calabro

121 Greek wig in bronze
(fifth century B.C.),
Reggio Museum

Gioia Tauro,
June 2, 1955

Twenty years ago in the company of Alessandro d'Entrèves, who then was teaching at Messina, I ferried over from that town to Reggio.

Reggio then made a poor impression, dusty, discoloured, sordid. The works of art I had come to see were dumped in a shed where I could not enjoy them. Nor, I confess, did I find any to enjoy.

We were not allowed to get away. I do not recall how it happened but against our will we were taken to a house where a sort of banquet of every sort of fruit and pastry and drink was piled up for our refreshment. We had to be obstinate, rude even, to wrench ourselves free from this overpowering hospitality in time to catch the ferry-boat back to Messina.

This time we came to spend the night and most of the following day, to see the sights.

To begin with let me say that Reggio now made a much better impression. A noble sea-front with gardens, animated broad streets rising in parallel terraces to fine public buildings. A feeling of intense life as at Catania across the water.

The sights are not many: the Angevin Castle and the museum where now are stored the Antique finds made in Calabria in recent years. Professor De Franciscis, the Superintendent of Antiquities for the whole region, took the trouble to have the museum opened for me in spite of its being a national holiday and guided us to the objects likely to interest an art lover rather than a professional archaeologist. I was greatly impressed by the marble head and feet and the bronze wig (unique of its kind, I believe) of a fifth-century statue, perhaps by the local sculptor Pythagoras of Rhegium.

I confess to enjoying even more a series of little terra-cotta tablets, like the predella panels of Italian altarpieces. All were ex-votos from a temple at Locri, dedicated to Persephone and most of them represent her rape by Hades. They differ in quality but the best are of as exquisite composition and contour as any other Greek low reliefs of about 500 B.C.

As we were leaving the Sovraintendente did not fail to utter the cry I hear wherever I go, the cry for funds to carry on, in this case the excavations in Locri and elsewhere in Calabria. But the welfare state of today undertakes so much

that when it comes to art it behaves like the middle-aged patient whose doctor warned him it was time to give up wine, women and song. He said he would begin with song. Did not even the British Museum a year or two ago propose to be open only in part and on alternate days to save an infinitesimal sum compared to what is being spent on defence and material welfare!

Except for the short visit to Reggio only twenty years ago, I had not returned to Calabria since May and June, 1908. The roads were then little more than tracks

Gioia Tauro,
June 3, 1955

145

full of holes covered up by deep pockets of dust, the inns unspeakable, not even Neolithic slums, food scarcely eatable. I recall dismal efforts at chewing and swallowing a tough leathery something called *genovese* which to my nose and palate smelled of old or aged ram or reverend he-goat. I rather dreaded returning to Calabria.

This time I found roads as pleasant as anywhere, nearly all asphalted and often hedged with beds of oleanders, geraniums, lavender. They wriggle and corkscrew over steep ascents and descents and you sweep from high pass to low valley a thousand metres in half an hour.

The little Jolly Hotels, successors to the ones started by Balbo at Jeffren, at Nalut, at Gadames in Tripolitania, offer every modern convenience and are so standardized that if you have been to one you know what to expect of any other. Of course the personal equation of management and attention cannot be eliminated, nor some dependence on local conditions for food and service. As a rule the management is in the hands of north Italians (again as in Balbo's hotels in North Africa) and chiefly from Trieste. In one case the director was of Bernese origin and his wife from Berlin. What waifs and strays hotel and restaurant personnel are! One seldom finds the same waiter after a season or two even in the most luxurious hostelries. They seem possessed by even more urge for change of place, for otherness than the rest of us. An elderly head-waiter with a face and expression as jovial and ironical as the English Punch confessed to having served on transatlantic liners, in restaurants and hotels in London, New York, Buenos Aires and now *per mio castigo* he found himself where we had the pleasure of enjoying his too brief acquaintance.

To return to the Jolly Hotels: their high American standard of comfort and the comparative inferiority of the food reminded me of what the president of a congress of French hotel-keepers proclaimed as recently as some twenty-five years ago: 'Nous ne rêvons pas à imiter les améliorations scatologiques des Anglo-Saxons mais nous insistons sur la bonne chère à laquelle nous autres Français sommes habitu's.' This president would not approve of the American standard of feeding and I would agree with him. It is due, in part at least, to the fact that in no other country do false teeth prevail so much as among us Americans and my own experience teaches me that with one's own teeth disappears much of the intelligent enjoyment of good food. Indeed, does not a popular American revivalist preacher of hygienic feeding begin his sermon by saying: 'Since it does not matter to you what you eat, you might as well stoke with things that are good for your health.'

Cosenza,
June 4, 1955

I did not read up for this tour of ten days in Calabria. Yet memory retains impressions of much history and travel perused many years ago. For instance

125 Edward Lear: 'View of Reggio', lithograph

the Reverend Tate Ramage, who early in the nineteenth century roamed in these parts in the summer, carrying a huge sunshade, dressed in white nankeen trousers and a frock-coat, the ample pockets of which contained his entire luggage. Or Lenormant with the treasure trove of distilled information of every kind about every place in Calabria as well as Apulia. Or Edward Lear, the painter who accompanied his lithographed landscapes with very subtle annotations on colour effects, on customs and inns and people. Gregorovius likewise and J. A. Symonds. And above all Norman Douglas's *Old Calabria*, now an English classic which, as Lenormant's *A travers l'Apulie et la Lucanie*, I have read again and again.[8] While it would not yield up definite dates or names, memory trailed —so to speak—tapestries, faded but fascinating, of historical association, digested, assimilated, forming part of me as no recent reading ever could.

So as we drove northward, this or that episode, this or that name connected with the Greek colonization of Calabria came into my mind, then the Germanic hordes on their way to Africa, and finally the Norman invasion synchronizing with the Norman conquest of England, and all the intestine struggles between the turbulent descendants of Tancred of Hauteville, devoured with lust for power and pelf, and the final triumph of Roger, the conqueror of Sicily.

126 Edward Lear: 'View of Scilla', lithograph

As we passed through Mileto I recalled that for some years it was politically as important as London or Paris and that its churches, palaces and treasures must have ranked with the best then being produced. All have disappeared in earthquakes that made the ground open and swallow up everything that stood on it.

Often do I wonder what excavation, when if ever it comes around to it, will bring to light marvellous buried treasures. Porphyry columns, capitals wind-swept or carved into baskets, coloured marbles of every kind, mosaics—in short all the best that Byzantine art at that time could furnish and probably superior to what still remains in and near Palermo.

I remember how in 1908, passing through the miserable village to which Mileto was reduced, we heard of what had just happened there: a priest poisoned in the chalice or stabbed to death at the moment of elevation.

At Cosenza where now a too up-to-date bridge, called Ponte Alarico, crosses the Busento I was stirred almost to tears as I recalled Platen's exquisitely evoca-tive verses about the burial of Alaric in the bottom of that stream. Carducci has translated them as well as possible, but the music of one language cannot be reproduced in another.

127 Edward Lear: 'View of Gerace', lithograph

But let me go back to our start from Reggio where, by the way, we were comfortably lodged and very well fed in a non-Jolly inn on the sea-front and in process of renovation. We drove along the sea, a riviera as beautiful as the Ligurian or French only not suburbanized, not contaminated by greased papers and empty cigarette packages, not overcrowded nor infested by advertisements as are so many stretches of the road along the sea from Marseilles to Livorno.

Gioia Tauro, our first stop, we choose not only because of its having a Jolly Hotel but so as to go to Gerace the next day. Leaving Gioia Tauro one passes through forests of olives as tall and graceful as elms. As we climbed these were succeeded by chestnuts and then by ilexes and finally by beeches. On reaching a height of almost 1,000 metres we came through a treeless high plateau of huge ferns and then only started plunging down towards our destination and into a very different world from the Tyrrhenian one. Few trees, no amenity, greyish white and reddish rocks of bold shape and very little arable land. On clear days the view of the coast towards Crotone and to Sicily opposite must be matchless but a heavy scirocco wrapped up everything in mist. Only the nearer heights of the Aspromonte were visible.

I cherished in memory the impression of Gerace on a golden May morning in

1908. The town still alive, the cathedral radiant with its procession of elegant Ionian columns along the spacious nave. Now the church was dreary and dusty under restoration and the town abandoned. Even the bishop has transferred himself to the thriving Locri down on the coast. A patent instance of the shuttle going backward and forward on the loom of time. Decline of prosperity, disinclination to work that was unremunerative, followed by malaria and piracy drove the remaining coast-dwellers to the heights. Now that healthful conditions and prosperity are returning to the shore it is the turn of the heights to be abandoned. It is foreseeable that in two or three decades Gerace will be as deserted as the exquisite town of Evenos high above Toulon in Provence.

But once the restoration of the cathedral is completed it will remain one of the rare sites of Italy that are perhaps even more nostalgically evocative through being no longer inhabited.

Cosenza,
June 6, 1955

Market day at Nicastro, where we lunched on our drive from Gioia to Cosenza, and a great many peasant women about selling and buying and in their traditional costume. An ample, closely pleated black skirt is lifted up over a red petticoat and tied into a great loop behind, thus forming a sort of 'panier'. It may be an eighteenth-century fashion still worn in this quiet corner. The majestic gait of these women is wonderfully accentuated by the movement of the panier.

After a drive through parklike mountain country, and a magnificent descent into the wide valley of the Crati, suddenly a town in an orgy of festivity. Arches pearled over with electric bulbs, crowds so packed that the car had to nuzzle its way through them, booths selling every kind of goods and every type of fancy rubbish. The following evening till nearly midnight, banging, bombing, bursting of fireworks. Beautiful as they scattered jewels of all colours in pear-shaped patterns. Must cost millions and millions of lire, easily collected we were told from the townsmen. No doubt some of it comes back through trade at the fair that for days draws the countryside. Streets full of young people bursting with health and good-looking, even handsome, all having a glorious time in ideally favourable weather.

The pretext for all this? The Feast of San Francesco of the neighbouring town of Paola.

Years and years ago, the younger Lacaita, the English son of the Risorgimento exile Sir James Lacaita, owner of an estate near Taranto, rejoicing still in the charming Greek name of Leucaspide, recounted how he had once been present

129, 130 Byzantine enamelled cross, Bishop's Palace, Cosenza

131 Head of the Madonna, detail from the Tomb of Isabella of Aragon, Cosenza Cathedral

at Paola itself during the celebration of its great saint. He heard cries of, 'Who is the real San Francesco? Is it San Francesco of Sales? No! Is it San Francesco Saverio? Never! Above all it is not that impostor, that pretender, that mischief-maker Francesco of Assisi! The only real San Francesco is our San Francesco, San Francesco of Paola'.

The old part of Cosenza is a noble town with a main street of stately palaces. In one of these, as our dear friend Count Tancredo Tancredi pointed out, was the birthplace of the Renaissance humanist Bernardino Telesio. In the cathedral the marble tomb of Isabella of Aragon (died 1270) with kneeling figures not Tuscan nor yet French but worthy of either school. In the Bishop's Palace a Byzantine cross said to have been brought back by Frederick *Stupor Mundi* from his crusade in Palestine. As enamel still of best artisanship but as drawing not quite of the same high quality. Perhaps done in Constantinople soon after its sack in 1204 and the flight of the more important artists.

In the afternoon our friends took us up to the Monte Scuro, the pass from which one looks across the high plateau of the Sila with its forests and pistachio green lakes to the bold outline of the mountain chain dividing it from the Ionian Sea. I was reminded of a fascinating dream landscape in an 'Assumption of the Virgin' by Matteo di Giovanni of Siena now in the National Gallery of London. How that reminder helped me to feel the particular quality of what I was looking at and how recalling it in the presence of the picture will enhance it for me!

132 Tomb of
Isabella of Aragon,
Cosenza Cathedral

On leaving Cosenza we went out of our way to see Altomonte Calabro before reaching Castrovillari. Country as empty as any in France but incomparably more dreamy and more romantic. Jagged mountains tending towards the pyramidal, and plains that thousands of years ago must have been lakes. Scarcely any farms to be seen and very few villages. All roads, even side roads, in excellent condition and clear indications at every turn. It stirred my envy as, except for the few asphalted highways, the roads I frequent from my house near Florence are almost everywhere in poor condition and consequently so dusty that if a car precedes one's own, driving becomes a distressing and even an exasperating pleasure. If only we had a *Cassa della Toscana* to remedy this and much else!

At last Altomonte appears, a real eyrie rising high over precipitous ravines. It is topped by a tower-like palace reminding one of the Palazzo Tolomei in Siena. The church in turn recalls modestly, ever so modestly, Santa Chiara in Naples. Behind the high altar a fine sepulchral monument of Filippo Sangineto, Count of Altomonte, by a follower of Tino di Camaino (plate 135), and over one of the outside portals a Madonna in the same Franco-Italian style as the one of Isabella of Aragon in Cosenza Cathedral.

Castrovillari not much more attractive than it was in 1908 but certainly much cleaner and through its Jolly Hotel it has become an excellent centre for excursions. How different from the loathsome lodgings I had to put up with in 1908! The next day through Spezzano Albanese with no Albanian costumes visible anywhere and through Terranova di Sibari with its enchanting view of the great half moon of mountains framing in the valley of the Crati; then skirting Corigliano Calabro we reached Rossano. An elegant little town high over the Ionian Sea full of Byzantine remains, none however of interest to a dilettante like me except the exquisite little church of San Marco (plate 120) crowning the other buildings. It is the cruciform structure with its tower-like dome that in various sizes exists all over the Orthodox Christian world from Vladimir and Suzdal in central Russia to the Caucasus and Armenia in the south and to rough rustic versions like those in Tarrasa in Catalonia and San Donato at Zara.

The most important sight of Rossano which for years I had been longing to see, the *Codex Purpureus Rossanensis*, has meanwhile been shown to me at the great exhibition of illuminated manuscripts in Italy held in Rome in 1953–4 and I did not even try this time to get any of the complicated permits necessary for obtaining access to it in the Bishop's Palace.

An inn with at least one spacious clean and comfortable room for my indispensable siesta and a *trattoria* run by a jolly ex-sailor who had been a prisoner in England and had brought back no resentment for the way he had been treated

133 Chiesa Madre,
Altomonte Calabro

there. We asked him whether there was anything in the rumour of the English-women having appreciated the company of the Italian prisoners so much and with a radiant smile he answered, 'Qualchecosa di vero ci potrebbe essere'. I enjoyed the cordial familiarity of our convives among themselves and the atmosphere of friendliness toward the passing stranger that one meets with so frequently in popular restaurants in Italy as nowhere else.

134 Santa Maria del Patirion, near Rossano Calabro

In the afternoon we drove up a precipitous road consisting entirely of hairpin turns with no parapets through a solitary *macchia* of ilex, yellow broom, myrtle, lentisk and laurel to the Basilian monastery of Patirion, no longer a home of prayer and meditation but serving the Forestry Department. Only the church remains, with a choir entirely Siculo-Arab as architecture, decorated with lozenge pattern in two colours, caramel and chocolate. The rather neglected interior has a floor mosaic, now dilapidated but originally perhaps as fine as the one in Otranto Cathedral.

The view ranging over the headlands towards Crotone and the coast of Sybaris to the Pollino group and other heights beyond. In clear weather I imagine the coast of Sicily may be visible too. During our trip the further distance was constantly veiled by summer mists.

The descent with the mountain on one side and hundreds of feet of precipice

135 Tomb of
Filippo Sangineto,
Chiesa Madre,
Altomonte Calabro

to the plain below alarmed me and I confess to a feeling of real relief when we reached the highroad and speeded back to Castrovillari.

As we passed again under the high-perched Corigliano we had to slow up because the road was crowded with people, the older ones on donkeys, the younger ones on bicycles or motorcycles or *lambrette*. Close by stood a huge billboard announcing that the fields we were passing had been reformed, that is to say allotted to the—I forget whether it said *contadini* or *agricoltori*. As I looked back at Corigliano I saw two or three or more huge buildings, high and portentous, just put up to house these beneficiaries of the land reform.

I am not a sociologist, politician, economist or philanthropist. But having been nearly everywhere in that problem-child of contemporary Italy, the Mezzogiorno, I venture to say that the real Mezzogiorno, that is to say Italy below Salerno and Lucera, suffers more from the absentee peasant than from the absentee landlord. True the latter spends the stingy income of his broad acres in Naples, Rome or even Monte Carlo or Paris. But much would be different if the Mezzogiorno had a peasantry, I mean people who from generation to generation live on a plot of ground, work it, love it, prefer it to any other spot on earth, even as Horace loved Taranto. In Tuscany it is not rare to find *poderi* that have been worked by the same family for over two hundred years. There are relatively very few real *contadini* in the Mezzogiorno. Instead there are agricultural labourers who used to walk miles to the plot of ground momentarily allotted to them, returning every evening to the huge slum agglomerations where they felt at home. At home in Neolithic conditions inconceivable to those who consider American comforts indispensable, but enjoying nevertheless life, real living, more, perhaps far more, than we do.

They are not being settled on the land. On this journey I have seen few cottages going up compared to the number of huge new barracks for agricultural labourers, providing vertical instead of horizontal slums.

Even if one tries to settle the agricultural labourer on the soil (I know it is being done in many regions and have seen very neat and promising looking cottages, particularly in Apulia) it will take two or even three generations before he becomes a peasant. Meanwhile he will feel wrenched from his habits, from his associates and the close contact with their excitements, their sorrows, their joys, all that made living taste like life. He will be unhappy, disgruntled and full of resentment against a government that means to do its best for him and will be ready to vote against it even without prompting from Soviet-minded agitators.

Praia a Mare,
June 9, 1955

On reaching Mormanno after the magnificent climb from Castrovillari with the view of the sombre pyramidal Pollino group on our right, the car came to a full stop. Luckily a garage was at hand and after less than an hour's delay we started again. Trouble like this with a car had not occurred for so long that I could not recall when it last happened. Memory went back to nearly fifty years ago when I never started out in a car without a time-table in my pocket on the probability that I should have to return by train. Mechanics were inadequate if regarded as domestics and not as sportsmen who condescended to serve you, and would frequently be unfit to drive because they had spent the night carousing or lechering. Then there was the lighting of the acetylene lamps which took forty to fifty minutes. And the roads! Even the great highways from Turin to Udine were apt to be, from October on, a marsh of mud and slush.

Wonderful descent to the coast by another precipitous road cut out of the rock and winding its way through a narrow defile. At Scalea we reached the new great highroad along the sea and soon after the Jolly Hotel of Praia a Mare, a prosperous small sea resort with a Homeric island opposite to it and enchanting view on the heights encircling the Gulf of Policastro. A good place for a day of complete rest and enjoyment of sea air and a spectacular sunset under the shelter of fabulously romantic rocks.

Our next stop for lunch, Vallo di Lucania, not too attractive, which may have been partly due to the rainy weather. A good *trattoria* but no hotel attached to it and we were sent to the so-called inn which looked to me like a broken-down palace of the time when provincial aristocracy still stayed at home. A bare but clean room was provided for my siesta, only before entering it I had to present my passport. I wonder what they made of it! The *trattoria* was ringing

*Naples,
June 11, 1955*

36 Mosaic floor (detail),
Santa Maria del Patirion,
near Rossano Calabro

with the merriment of the small children of the cook-proprietor. A real *bottegone* scene which Velasquez and Picaresque novels have taught me to appreciate.

Then on through magnificent chestnut woods and longing to take the roads that we saw turning off to the headland of Palinuro and to Velia. At my age my motto has got to be, 'Entbehren sollst Du, Du sollst entbehren', for many are the things I have to give up to spare my strength. I should gladly have seen Velia again, the Elea of the Eleatic school of philosophy to which it offered a worthy situation.

Suddenly far below us the sparkling sea and what did my eyes behold? More romantic than the first glimpse of Segesta as you approach it from the north, are the temples of Paestum. One of the most magical and promising visions I ever beheld. As we drew near I was distressed to find the temple area surrounded by barbed wire, and instead of the feeling hitherto experienced of the remote, the long ago in time, automobiles in numbers with hordes of tourists pouring out of them.

The new museum houses relatively few finds from Paestum itself and all that was dug up in and around the Heraeum of the Foce del Sele.

It seems to me a great pity in a way not to leave these finds in that enchanting meadow close to the river, with its wooded banks and the branches of huge old cork oaks dipping into the green current. To the waterless Greek pioneers it must have seemed a paradise. Even to me years ago when Zanotti Bianco kindly invited me to come and see what, after reading a few words of Strabo, he had the vision, the courage and the persistent endurance to carry through, that clearing in the forest near the river's mouth suggested a spot like the one Odysseus landed on and heard Calypso singing at her loom.

Then the Archaic metopes were still lying about in the open or in sheds and the serious student could discover and enjoy them for himself without being jostled by bored and weary tourists.

Possibly the reconstruction of a Doric temple such as the Heraeum once was would have been a better solution than the present one for housing the various finds. The metopes would have found their proper place and the other objects could have been adequately shown in the interior. But perhaps the decline from poetry to archaeology is inevitable.

*

My long-cherished dream of revisiting Calabria has been realized even if sites that I longed to see again like Stilo and Crotone have had to be cut out from my programme. Though poor in monuments and works of art as compared to other regions of Italy it is one of the finest in its classical severity, its wide prospects of utterly unspoilt landscape and one of the most delightful to visit and even to linger in.

II Apse of Sant'Apollinare in Classe, Ravenna,
with the 'Transfiguration' in mosaic (middle of sixth century A.D.)

137   Sant'Apollinare in Classe, Ravenna

III 'The Emperor Justinian I with his Suite and Archbishop Maximian', mosaic
(middle of sixth century A.D.), San Vitale, Ravenna

138 Mosaic in the Mausoleum of Galla Placidia, Ravenna

Ravenna,
September 18, 1955

Left Vallombrosa yesterday to come here. Radiant but crisp weather, sky crystal clear, landscape like a cosmic illuminated page. From Pontassieve to Dicomano almost a continuous suburb, a gay prosperous one. Busy traffic on the Muraglione road. Towns, after eight years since we were in these parts, so grown on outskirts, so bustling with activity as to be unrecognizable. Again I ask: Italy, where is your so much publicized poverty? The contrast between sun and shade, except in midsummer, is startling in Italy. I look at old palaces glowing in the sun but I know from experience how icy and cheerless they are within, out of the sunshine. Is something like that possible with the economic aspect of things? That behind the bustle, the fervid activity, the shops, the crowded cafes and restaurants, there is a shady side—not shady in the moral but in the economic sense—that is known only to economists, to philanthropists?

Ravenna,
September 19, 1955

The kind, the epoch, the school used to absorb me so much that the individual work of art lost its specificity in my affection. I used to know all that was known about, *about* what, about *it*? No, about the genre, early Christian, Byzantine,

Romanesque, Gothic. I threw my entire self into one or the other of these and lived each in succession. It, the individual, the specific work of art was a needle in the haystack of the genre. Indeed I never asked whether, apart from the *about*, there was an *it*. Now, here at Ravenna, for instance, I discover that I have forgotten most of the *about*. It has grown dim and vague, reduced to a mere atmosphere. The result is that only the objects that have an *it*, a quality within a style, remain. So yesterday I was overwhelmed by the space of San Vitale (colour plate III), the mosaics of Galla Placidia, the nave and the sarcophagi of

139 Mausoleum of
Galla Placidia, Ravenna

Sant'Apollinare in Classe (colour plate II and plate 137), the severe and precise masonry of Theodoric's tomb, his porphyry sarcophagus, all as sheer
beauty. Yet I have not lost what makes up most of the *about*, the perspective, the
distances of or in time. Without them I should be like so many practising
artists who judge a thing by what appeals to them, their caprice and their
problems exclusively, unable to allow for the awkwardness, uncouthness,
but also naïveté and candour of immaturity. I have lost facts, lost names, lost
nearly everything that constitutes the *about*, nearly all except the perspective and
procession of time which is really the sense that makes culture. The cultivated
person places everything in perspective of time. It is never out of his mind and it
affects not only works of art but also current events.

And what is history if not *temps retrouvé*? It is the autobiography of the human
race in general and, for us Europeans, of ours in particular. Everything that has
led up to us since we became human. Events that have not affected our growth
or led up to significantly dynamic events are mere chronicle as distinct from
history. Even a chronicle does not comprise remotely all that has happened.
Most happenings remain unrecorded even by the daily, the hourly press. Therefore history can never pretend to record all that has happened. It can try to guess,
and the best guesses rely on the intuition, on the imagination of the historian, on
the perspective he gives to the events that impose themselves and that he surrep-
titiously selects for his epoch. Real history, as distinguished from chronicle,
cannot avoid being epic, good or bad but epic. More than pseudo-philosophy
and pretentious generalizations, a significant anecdote evokes the past and
characterizes individuals who have been engaged in influencing and shaping it.
History is not something that inexorably marches on regardless of mankind. On
the contrary, it is composed of the history of individual creeds, passions, follies,
heroisms in contrast with a universe that knows us not and goes its own way.
The account of how man has managed to subdue this outer world to his needs,
to his pleasures, to his ideals, the struggle to master nature, to exploit it despite
nature's utter indifference, is a great chapter of history. So is anything that has
helped to humanize us, to give us command of our passions, to feel for others.
Art history likewise, properly understood, is not one of mere happenings to
artists and to their creations.

Ravenna,
September 20, 1955

In June, 1889, when I first came here, Ravenna seemed to lie at the bottom of
the sea of time, almost as silent as the grave. A footfall made an echo. Now it is
hustling with terrific traffic, bicycles lining the roads like a solid barrier, every
kind of motor vehicle dashing backwards and forwards, torrents of sturdily
vital people, policemen directing the traffic, huge ponderous office buildings
offending the sky-line.

The same in Rimini where we had not been since 1947. I then went there on
purpose to see with my own eyes what the bomb damage to the Tempio
Malatestiano had been. The Superintendent of Fine Arts came over from
Ravenna to meet me and together we looked at the building, its right wall
dangerously inclined and out of plumb. He explained that the only way of

141 West wall of the Tempio Malatestiano, Rimini

saving it would be to take down the masonry stone by stone, numbering them and then reconstructing it. He seemed frightened by the gigantic task and very timid about undertaking it. As we were looking at the façade a deputation appeared headed by the bishop and the mayor of the town who, knowing that I had been successful in getting 50,000 dollars from the Kress Foundation for the restoration of the Tempio, wanted me to support them in not having it done. They kept urging that the community was impatient to worship in its own cathedral, that so radical a restoration might change the wanted aspect of the cherished temple, that the marble blocks taken down one by one might end by crumbling. I got the clear impression that what they really wanted was to have the money available for other things and I had great difficulty in not losing my temper altogether. Fortunately the Direzione Generale in Rome did not pay the slightest attention to these complaints and hesitations and had the work carried through magnificently. It made me happy to see it completed and to find Piero della Francesca's fresco of Sigismondo Malatesta well placed and lit in a chapel by itself.

Ferrara,
September 21, 1955

Spent an hour in the Palazzo dei Diamanti and found the picture gallery dreary and abandoned, the paintings, with very few exceptions, disappointing. Their glory has departed with the zest I had for classifying them. During the time I was there only one other visitor appeared. In the magnificent courtyard some fine late Antique fragments and sarcophagi attracted my attention. In a corner I discovered a sign, 'Museo Boldini', a glory of Ferrara. What would have become of him if he had remained there and never gone to Paris? Got a guard to open two or three spacious rooms where were exhibited some good

142, 143 Giovanni Boldini: Two sketches for portraits, Museo Boldini, Ferrara

etchings, several sketches for portraits and other unrepresentative paintings, his palette, etc., and the Empire furniture of his bedroom. I knew him well. Disagreeable, rather dandiacal personality, looked as if he had a nasty taste in his mouth. As artist, ultra-chic, particularly when portraying elongated society ladies painted as if with translucent glass, very taking and with a certain dash and pep even.

Could not resist the temptation of getting back to Pomposa. Its monumental bell-tower rose mysteriously over the fertile plain with its long lines of poplar trees just as it used to when I first approached it in a lumbering landau on a hot

Ferrara,
September 22, 1955

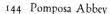

summer day many decades ago. When we got near there was a change even here. The new high road from Venice to Ravenna passes close by and a party of tourists were packing into a motor bus just as we drove up. It is not the same world-forgotten, dream-like place any longer, but as shadows lengthened and the buildings and tower glowed in the sunset light, I was able to recapture some of the old enchantment.

145   Master of the Castello 'Nativity': 'Annunciation', San Giovannino dei Cavalieri, Florence

Instead of wandering to distant lands as I have been doing for many years during the early summer months, I have stayed in Florence and dedicated what little energy I still muster to renewing my acquaintance with the inexhaustible art treasures of Florence and to discovering my present relations to them.

My first task has been to see the Uffizi again and luckily Filippo Rossi, the Superintendent of Fine Arts, has granted me permission of entry on days when the gallery is shut to the public so that I can have it all to myself. A privilege I am deeply grateful for.

Found the first half completely theatralized. The effect is startling and fetch-ing. Do the inventors of this flashy way of exhibiting them regard works of art as incapable of inviting attention when left to themselves? The greatest of them talk not with the storm, not with thunder and lightning, but with a still, small voice. Perhaps it takes an Elijah to hear it and the tourists in chain gangs 'peritortized' through the bowels and halls of a museum are scarcely Elijahs; nor, if they were, could they enjoy the leisure of spirit, or indeed in the hustling crowd, yelled at by guides, see and feel. All is now done to hustle them through museums, not to teach or enlighten them.

146 Paolo Uccello: 'The Drunkenness of Noah' (detail), detached fresco from the Chiostro Verde, Santa Maria Novella, Florence

To the Pitti where the curator, Anna Maria Ciaranfi, receives me most hos-pitably on the day of *chiusura* and leaves me to wander about *à la recherche du temps perdu*. Only unlike Proust's re-encountered old friends, the faces and expressions are the same I looked at first nearly seventy years ago. I hear friends complain of the 'old-fashioned' arrangement of the Pitti Gallery. To my eye it is entirely satisfactory. The jewels, the real masterpieces stand out clearly against a background of less important paintings. The effect is of a collection made by lovers of pictures and not by salesmen and showmen. It is to the credit of the Florentine Fine Art Administration that the old order has been respected as an historical monu-ment of taste.

147 Master of the Castello 'Nativity': 'Miracle of St Benedict', detached fresco from the cloisters of the Badia, Florence

Accompanied by Ugo Procacci to a large sort of workshop near Buontalenti's grotto in the Boboli Gardens where various important detached frescoes are being admirably cleaned and restored. First and foremost Uccello's 'Deluge' and 'Drunkenness of Noah' from the Chiostro Verde. In both, but particularly in the 'Deluge', the whole composition with its astonishing effects of perspective is now clearly visible. Sad only that they cannot be put back where they belong. Fascinating the series of episodes from the life of St Benedict that used to be in

148 Master of the Castello 'Nativity': Leading lines under the 'Miracle of St Benedict', Badia, Florence

149 Bronzino: 'Laura Battiferri',
Loeser Bequest, Palazzo Vecchio, Florence

150 Tino di Camaino: Angel,
Loeser Bequest, Palazzo Vecchio, Florence

the Chiostro degli Aranci at the Badia. Procacci assures me that documents revealing the name of the author and his dates must exist in the Florentine archives and that if only he was less pressed for time he could find them. Granted, but it would not teach us much more than we know already. The group to which these frescoes belong is clearly defined, clustering around the charming 'Nativity' formerly at Castello. The Master of the Castello 'Nativity', as I call him, must have been a close follower of Fra Angelico, influenced later by Fra Filippo and later still by Filippo's son, Filippino.

Turning round I noticed a heap of what looked to me like grey, dusty carpets or tapestries. 'What are these?' 'Alas, frescoes that had to be detached all over Florence and that cannot be restored for lack of funds.' It is surprising that if considerable funds were available for the not urgently necessary new arrangement of the Uffizi there should be none for prolonging the life of these precious invalids. The Soprintendenza plans to place them eventually in the convent of the Carmine, calling it a museum of frescoes. Much as I regret their having to be torn from the places they were made for, this would seem the least bad solution.

To the Badia, with not a soul to disturb one's enjoyment of the Mino, the Filippino, and the Chiostro degli Aranci with the drawings remaining on the walls after the frescoes have been removed (plate 148). Elegance of every column, big and little, and vitality of all carving.

To the Palazzo Vecchio where Giovanni Poggi, not being able to accompany us himself, delegated his assistant, Ispettore Cirri, to guide us through this astonishing rabbit warren and to show us all the recent restorations and discoveries. He took us through passages and rooms, some with exquisite ceilings, that I did not remember ever seeing before. Found the Loeser Bequest well displayed but, except for a few outstanding works of art like the Tino di Camaino angel and the Bronzino portrait of Laura Battiferri, less interesting than I remembered it. Or was I already too tired? There is too much to be taken

151 Sala dei Gigli after restoration, Palazzo Vecchio, Florence

in for one visit and we had to leave Eleonora's Studiolo for next time. But I was glad to see with my own eyes how much has been done under Poggi's discriminating direction.

Back to the Uffizi to see the new arrangement of fifteenth- and sixteenth-century rooms. Walls too white, pictures tend to be shown off as if being auctioned rather than allowed to speak for themselves. Yet on the whole the visibility has been increased and many are better accompanied, Botticelli especially well brought together. One is allowed to step back until the space relations and the depths of the 'Primavera' are fully revealed. Opposite to it, Hugo van der Goes's triptych (I am not sure I enjoy the harsh contrast between such an actual and such an ideal world) takes one's breath away—the bundle of straw in the foreground, the vase with the iris, the white damask of female robes, and above all the winter landscape. You feel like plunging a thermometer into it to measure the degrees of frost. No more precise drawing has ever been done, and in Europe none more refined and more delicate. Only Botticelli can be more subtle with more significant contours.

The traffic in the streets is frightening for one so little used to going into town. I generally arrive by car at my destination in a panic and am relieved if the driver can manage to stop without my having to cross a street. Maybe late at night or in the first morning hours one could still indulge in such old-fashioned pursuits as sauntering along, stopping in the middle of the street to stare up at façades of palaces and churches, meditating and dreaming. On the other hand, when one has just left the street with its noise and bustle, the quietness not only inside the churches but in the open cloisters at Santa Maria Novella, at San Lorenzo, in the Badia is almost unbelievable. Only a faint distant hum seems to reach these enchanted spaces.

The silence in these cloisters, which prevailed in the Middle Ages at least as much as now, makes one realize how easy it was in those noisy and over-crowded medieval towns to take refuge in them and to live a life of tranquil concentration.

To the Accademia on an ordinary day and surprised to find it too relatively empty. One would expect the unique group of Michelangelo's sculptures to attract vast crowds even if the paintings, except for the Lorenzo Monacos, perhaps the Ghirlandaio and one or two quaint pictures of the fourteenth century, can only be of interest to the attributor. Same with most shows of Italian paintings, like the Pontormos at the Palazzo Strozzi or the 'Primitifs' now exhibited in the Orangerie in Paris. Precious few in either would attract one for their own

152 Studiolo of Eleonora after restoration, Palazzo Vecchio, Florence

qualities. The boiling interest is in questions of who did them and whose attribution is the right and whose the wrong one. Hence falsification of values and
corruption of taste are not as of old naively, but deliberately produced nowadays.
Exhibitionitis is a disease and not merely a figurative one. It should be put under
control like other contagious diseases. Instead I learn that forty of Italy's choicest
paintings are soon to be trundled forward and backward to Washington and
New York.⁹

Yesterday to the Ognissanti Church. Looked at Botticelli's 'St Augustine'. No
picture of an intellect engaged on the highest problems compares with this, not

even Dürer's, Michelangelo's or Rembrandt's. Realized plastically as draftsman-
ship, modelling in colour, all in a most communicative way. Appurtenances
painted with accuracy and understanding of what a thinking writer wants near
him. And yet how little known, even to a cultivated public, and how unappre-
ciated! Curious, considering that Botticelli is among the favourites of the pre-
sumable art lovers. Until Rossetti and Ruskin and English Pre-Raphaelites,
and particularly Pater, discovered him he was scarcely known. Even Burckhardt gave him scant attention, and other writers of nearly a hundred years ago,

154 Michelangelo:
'Pietà' (detail),
Florence Cathedral

if they mentioned him at all, spoke of him as inferior to Ghirlandaio. Owing no doubt to Pater, I loved him at sight though it took decades before I understood him.

To the Duomo. Had a good look at Michelangelo's 'Pietà' and was struck by two comparisons: one that the composition as a whole is based on the 'Laocoön', the other that the head of the Nicodemus is a self-portrait. I do not mean to say or imply that Michelangelo deliberately copied the 'Laocoön' or deliberately portrayed himself in the Nicodemus. More likely he was unaware of doing either. Even great artists do their best unconsciously. I cited in my *Aesthetics and History* (or was it elsewhere?) the case of Matisse whom I reproached for being too Cambodian. He was genuinely amazed and denied my charge. I asked him to look at the walls of his studio bristling with cases of Cambodian reliefs. A young man, back from a long stay at Olympia, brought drawings that reeked of its sculptures and was distressed beyond words when I said they were good copies of them. He swore it was his natural way of seeing.

Forty years ago I horrified fellow-students of the art of the past by asking wherein Michelangelo as sculptor and sculptor only was other or more than a Pergamon artist reborn, or the result of a kindred or parallel evolution. I ask the same question still. The only answer I can give to explain the esteem in which he is held, while the Pergamon school is treated with a certain contempt, is that as an illustrator, and for us Christians both begotten and formed by Christianity, as culture, Michelangelo appeals through his tragically sublime feeling for life, through the divine discontent expressed in his marbles, through their brooding sense of things unborn. In short, it is as an illustrator that he appeals over-whelmingly and as artisan. He could imply and deeply express in stone what he had to communicate—although not all that he meant to communicate.

My love for the Master of the Castello 'Nativity' has led me back to San Giovannino dei Cavalieri in Via San Gallo to reacquaint myself with a delight-ful 'Annunciation' of his (plate 145). It shows already the influence of Filippino and must therefore be a late work. Found the church beautifully kept by a young parish priest who seems to care passionately for the works of art belonging to it. He has even managed to have a fine Lorenzo Monaco 'Crucifixion' returned from the Uffizi depot to its former place behind the altar.

Happy to find the great Masaccio fresco in Santa Maria Novella admirably restored and in its own place. Did not remember the astonishing *trompe l'œil* of an altar on which the Crucifix seems to rest now with the painting of the skeleton underneath it.

The Chiostro Verde as attractive as ever and the drawings that have appeared under the detached Uccello frescoes well worth studying. Yet I feel nostalgic for the days when these frescoes were still in their place and tolerably visible.

To the Ufficio del Restauro to look at paintings in process of restoration. X-rays, '*sinopie*', *pentimenti*; the discovery of the painful gestation of the work of art destroys all aesthetic as contrasted with cerebral pleasure. It is the same as the various attempts at getting back to an Ur-Homer or an Ur-Pentateuch. One

155 Masaccio: 'The Holy Trinity with two Donors', fresco, Santa Maria Novella, Florence

156 Lorenzo Monaco: 'Marriage of the Virgin' (detail),
fresco, Santa Trinita, Florence

157 Lorenzo Monaco: 'Nativity of the Virgin'
(detail), fresco, Santa Trinita, Florence

ceases to enjoy them as literature or to take them as history, if only as *Historia Romanca*. One gets absorbed in the how or the why, having no interest in the what. All becomes mere philology. I would almost prefer to see a painting in no matter how bad a condition and dream of how much better it must have been once upon a time than have it torn to pieces the way philologists tear to pieces Homer, the Bible and other ancient texts. Time lays its hand on anything man does and more often as artist than as distorter.

Wherever we go I find great improvements in the system of lighting up pictures and frescoes, as for instance in the Brancacci Chapel at the Carmine (frontispiece) or the Lorenzo Monaco chapel at Santa Trinita. There is only the disadvantage that the good light shows deterioration, dust and dirt almost too harshly. The enchanting frescoes by Lorenzo Monaco at Santa Trinita, among the loveliest of the early Quattrocento, are fast disappearing. Could nothing be done to save them?

By no means all the sights of Florence are overcrowded, for many of them do not figure in the obligatory tourist programme. If you want to be undisturbed go to the Chiostro dello Scalzo, with the chiaroscuro wall-paintings by Andrea del Sarto, to the Castagno Museum, to the Innocenti Pinacoteca, to the Bardini Museum (so attractive in its well displayed variety of medieval sculpture, art objects and Persian rugs) and above all to the incomparable Horne Museum. Incomparable not so much on account of its contents, interesting and worth studying as they may be, but for the purity of its architecture. I know no better

158 Loggia,
Museo Horne, Florence

example of a Florentine Renaissance interior in which one still could live with modern comforts.

Opera del Duomo, renovated and now having as its chief attraction not only the two *cantorie*, one by Donatello and the other by Luca della Robbia, but Donatello's statues from the Campanile where they no longer could stand exposure to weather. Although we have no monumental figures by della Robbia, he was to a degree rare since the fourth century B.C. a sculptor through and through, while Donatello always impresses me as a painter with clay or stone or bronze instead of with pencil or pigment. How I wish I could make this as clear to others as it is to myself. I am intuitive and gnomic, at times epigrammatic, but have no gift for exposition, for finding entry into a recalcitrant mind.

159 Donatello: Cantoria (detail), Opera del Duomo, Florence

160 Luca della Robbia: Cantoria (detail), Opera del Duomo, Florence

Back to the Accademia to have another look at the overwhelmingly impressive
unfinished Michelangelos and at the 'Palestrina Pietà'. In this group the right
arm of Christ seems enormous while the thighs are far too thin, the heave of the
chest and abdomen utterly exaggerated. Head and face suggest advanced Sei-
rather than early Cinquecento and yet, and yet? It somehow reeks of Michelangelo and if not by him it must be by somebody who meant to be taken for

him. Could it be Bernini as has been suggested? The whole group did not impress me, persuade me, convince me, as do the figures of the slaves struggling to escape the matter in which they are engaged.

Received by Giulia Sinibaldi and her young assistant Maria Fossi in the print-room at the Uffizi where they eagerly show me the excellent new installation, the

facilities for students, the lighting and heating arrangements. How I wish I were able to take advantage of it all. The contrast with the cold discomfort I used to find there in my early days is almost comical.

Driving up to San Miniato across the Piazzale Michelangelo makes me recall what was reported to me, by a learned friend who had to accompany him, about Hitler's gazing at the famous view and exclaiming, 'At last I understand

164 Pulpit, San Miniato, Florence ▶

Boecklin!' The relation of this very classical view to anything as romantic and sensual as Boecklin is no more absurd perhaps than Hitler's politics, so largely responsible for the purgatorial state of the world in which we now palpitate.

In contrast to so much confusion of thought what order, what clarity, what distinction, what subtlety of composition, what delicacy of moulding in the façade of San Miniato! It anticipates all that is best in a Quattrocento design and makes one wonder whether, but for the Gothic invasion, Quattrocento architecture would not have flowered much earlier.

Inside the space is still rather medieval with a choir high over a crypt as, for instance, in the cathedral of Modena. Enchanting the exquisite lace-like patterns on the floor here as in the Baptistery at Florence. Fascinating the statue, as thickset and concentrated as a Sumerian one, that sustains the lectern of the pulpit. Of unsurpassable elegance the carving of all the cornices in a style almost confined to Florence. The walls of the nave covered with frescoes not done with an ornamental purpose but as ex-votos, pell-mell and one over the other. Near the entrance a colossal St Christopher in early Romanesque style reminding one of similar figures in northern Italy. Probably the work of a pilgrim painter.

A perfect specimen of pure Quattrocento art, the chapel built for the tomb of a young Portuguese cardinal, is now permanently closed and I wonder with what purpose. There is nothing in it that free access could disturb or damage. Is it mainly a question of 'baksheesh'?

A youthful novice led us to the upper cloister to see the nearly effaced frescoes of Paolo Uccello. If I remember my Vasari right, the artist did not quite finish them because he got too bored with the monotonous food the monks provided for him. What strikes one about these sadly damaged scenes is the way they remind one of Donatello. How little respect artists of one period had for their colleagues of the previous one is shown by a late sixteenth-century fresco over one of Uccello's.

Invited by Mario Gobbo, the head of the Azienda del Turismo, and by Piero Bargellini, the Assessore Comunale for Fine Art, to visit the Fortezza del Belvedere, a fortress at the very top of the town, commanding Florence and all its approaches to prevent any attempt of insiders and outsiders to get rid of Cosimo I, Duke of Florence. Employing engineers at a time when they still could not help being artists, he created an edifice that was architecture and sculpture combined and not a mere machine for a given purpose. The Comune with the financial help of the Azienda del Turismo has managed to dislodge the military from it, to do away with later outbuildings and sheds, and to free the monumental walls from the encumbering ramparts of earth. The work of restoration is still going on in the central building under the direction of the architect

Nello Bemporad. Soon it will be one of the finest sights of Florence. We enjoyed it on a late afternoon with the purest sky and all the way to the horizon every detail in the landscape appeared as in an illuminated fifteenth-century manuscript. The novelty of seeing so clearly, so minutely, was positively life-enhancing; and how I delighted in the proportions, the masonry, the mouldings, the relief of all artifacts.

With Procacci to the Villa Carducci at Legnaia to see the remains there of Castagno's frescoes now at Sant'Apollonia. A compound of Trecento and Quattrocento buildings that must once have been a commodious patrician country house. Now occupied by peasants and artisans except for the rooms with the frescoes. Best preserved is a fine figure of Eve, as lovely as anything Castagno ever did. On the outside a window facing east witnesses to what the whole building must have been. Its cornices and mouldings are of the best quality, inspired by the Antique, like so much architecture seen in Florentine mid-Quattrocento painting and in Ferrarese imitations of it.

To San Martino alla Palma, one of the rare spots on earth where in appropriate weather one feels art and nature to be in perfect harmony. I call the church with

166 Loggia of San Martino alla Palma, Scandicci

167 Andrea del Castagno: 'Eve', fresco, Villa Carducci, Legnaia

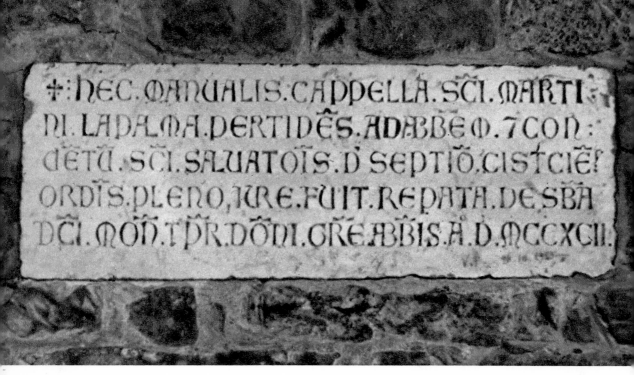

168 Medieval inscription, San Martino alla Palma, Scandicci

its colonnades 'a rustic Parthenon'. The material is of the most ordinary, common grey limestone and wood, but the columns are so exquisitely spaced, so delicately carved as to produce the effect of refined frames for the pictures furnished by the actual landscape. This too is a miracle. Fully sculptural hills more or less pyramidal, or at least triangular, rising up in places to 2,000 feet from a perfectly horizontal plain. The contrast between the pure geometry of the plain and the movement of the hills with their long, downward sloping lines is infinitely reposeful.

Leaving the Loggia I am again struck by a dedicatory inscription of the thirteenth century, one of the most beautiful pieces of medieval lettering known to me.

Drove back yesterday from Pratolino along the vast stretch of park walls and then across the Via Faentina to Fiesole. The landscape was stretching westward and southward in early summer's prime, yellow and green and gold, the distant horizons merely horizontal, and in between the sharp cut of the Mugnone valley under Fiesole and beyond it Florence itself like a mirage. But for *Wanderlust* where else, what distant climes would offer more appealing, more captivating scenery? Of course not the sublime spectacle of the Himalayas or the Alps. Everything more *à la mesure de l'homme* and thereby more satisfactory.

1 (*Rome, May 20 1947:* Page 18) In every probability it represents Tamar chased out of the Royal Palace by Amnon. See 2 Sam. xiii. 18–19.

2 (*Rome, October 29, 1950:* Page 25) It has been published since this was written. See Ludwig Budde, 'Severisches Relief im Palazzo Sacchetti', *Jahrbuch des Deutschen Archaeologischen Instituts* (Ergänzungsheft 80), Berlin, 1955.

3 (*Rome, November 25, 1952:* Page 31) It has now been returned to the new Palestrina Museum.

4 (*Messina, May 21, 1953:* Page 70) It is now back at Dresden.

5 (*Messina, May 21, 1953:* Page 70) See *Cronache d'Arte*, Bologna, 1924, page 254.

6 (*Enna, May 28, 1953:* Page 82) Since then several other interesting mosaics and other fragments have been dug up and, most interesting of all, an inscription proving that the villa was built and inhabited by Maximian, one of the tetrarchs represented in the porphyry group at Venice. See Gino Vinicio Gentili, *La Villa Romana di Piazza Armerina* (Itinerari dei Musei e Monumenti d'Italia 87), 2nd edition, Rome, 1954.

7 (*Palermo, June 12, 1953:* Page 120) It has since been transferred to the newly arranged museum of medieval and Renaissance sculpture and painting in the Palazzo Abbatelli, Palermo.

8 (*Cosenza, June 4, 1955:* Page 147) When I wrote these lines in 1955 George Gissing's account of his trip to Calabria in 1897 had slipped from my memory. The new edition (*By the Ionian Sea*, The Richards Press, London, 1956) made me realize again what a gifted writer and acute observer this bitter pessimist was, and how prodigious his familiarity with classical literature and history.

9 (*Florence:* Page 175) The project was finally dropped after violent protests from all sides.

Index

Roman numerals refer to colour plates
Numbers in italic refer to black-and-white illustrations

Aqueduct of Claudius, *1*
Acragas, *see* Agrigento
Agrigento, 64, 98–106, 128; *72*
    Altar of the Chthonic Deities, *78*
    Cathedral, 101, 102; *74, 77*
    Museum, 102; *75, 76*
    Rupe Atenea, 102
    Temple of Concord, 104; *73, 79*
    Temple of Zeus, 102; *75, 76*
Alaric, 95, 148
Alatri, 23
Alban hills, 18
Altomonte Calabro, 154
    Chiesa Madre, 154; *133, 135*
Andrea del Sarto, 181
Angelico, Fra, 86, 172
Annibaldi, Canon Giovanni, 46
Anselmi, Anselmo, 46
Antique art, 20, 22, 25, 31–2, 70, 79, 90, 102–6,
    108, 113, 117–18, 142, 166, 190
Antonello da Messina, 70–2, 88; *47, 48, 49*
Antwerp, Musée Royal, 70; *49*
Argentina, 130, 140
Aspendus, 74
Aspromonte, 149
Assisi, San Francesco, 126
Athens, 64, 102, 106
    Parthenon, 101, 106, 111, 192
    Propylaea, 106

Baalbek, 34, 136, 137
Bagheria, 122
    Villa Palagonia, 122, 127; *99, 100*
    Villa Valguarnera, 122
Balbo, Italo, 146
Baldovinetti, Alessio, 71
Barbantini, Nino, 41
Bargellini, Piero, 188
Baroque art, 70, 88, 98; *89*
Basaiti, Marco, 56
Bassae, 111

Bastiani, Lazzaro, 39–40
Battiferri, Laura, 173; *149*
Bellini, Gentile, 64; *40*
Bellini, Giovanni, 46, 56, 71, 72, 140
Bemporad, Nello, 190
Bergamo, 40, 42, 44
    Santa Maria Maggiore, *24*
Berlin, 56, 136, 146
Bernini, 185
Bissolo, Pier-Francesco, 56
Boecklin, Arnold, 188
Boldini, Giovanni, 166–7; *142, 143*
Bologna, 48
Bottari, Stefano, 72, 95
Botticelli, Sandro, 18–20, 34, 174, 175–6; *58*
Brandard, Edward, *63, 103*
Bronte, 79
Bronzino, Angelo, 173; *149*
Brydone, Patrick, 95
Budde, Ludwig, 193
Burckhardt, Jakob, 176
Busento river, 95, 148
Byzantine art, 54, 58–64, 71, 92, 148, 152, 154,
    162

Cagliostro, Alessandro, 127
Cairo, 137, 139
Calabria
    Agricultural reform and peasants, 158
    Books about, 146–7
    History of, 147–8
Calascibetta, 80; *55*
Cambodian art, 178
Caputo, Giacomo, 130, 132, 134, 136
Caravaggio, 27, 52, 54, 56, 70
Carducci, Giosuè, 148
Carrière, Eugène, 24
Casale, 80
    Mosaics, 81–4, 86; *56, 57, 60*
Castagno, Andrea del, 181, 190; *167*
Castello, 172

Castello 'Nativity', Master of the, 172, 178; *145, 147, 148*

Castelvetrano, 106, 108
  Municipio, *82*

Castrovillari, 154, 158

Catania, 72, 76, 78, 79, 130

Cefalù, 64
  Museum, *47*

Cézanne, Paul, 72, 80

Charles V, Emperor, 88

Christus, Petrus, 72

Ciaranfi, Anna Maria, 170

Cicogna, Anna Maria (daughter of Giuseppe Volpi), 130, 134

Cini, Count Vittorio, 41, 42

Cirri, Giulio, 173

Claude Lorraine, 36

Colonna, Vittoria, 98

Conspicuous waste, 53

Constantine, 82, 52

Constantinople, 52, 62, 108, 152
  Church of the Apostles, 60, 120
  Fatimieh Mosque, *see* Church of the Apostles
  Karieh Djami, 64
  St Sophia, 60

Cordova
  Cathedral, 140
  Palace of San Jeronimo, 92

Corigliano Calabro, 154, 158

Corot, Jean-Baptiste-Camille, 36

Cosenza, 95, 146, 149, 150, 152, 154
  Bishop's Palace, 152; *129, 130*
  Cathedral, 152, 154; *131, 132*
  Ponte Alarico, 148

Cosimo I, 188

Cousen, John, 72, *85, 102*

Crati river, 151, 154

Credaro, 43

Cyrene, 92, 130

Daniele da Volterra, *153*

Davies, William, 26

Decamps, Gabriel-Alexandre, 138

Deformation of words, 76-8

De Franciscis, Alfonso, 142

De Gasperi, Alcide, 70

Delacroix, Ferdinand-Victor-Eugène, 138

De Roberto, Federico, 78

Desiderio da Settignano, 88

Directoire style, 120

Donatello, 32, 182, 188; *159*

Douglas, Norman, 147

Dresden, 70, 193

Dürer, Albrecht, 176

Economic conditions in Italy, 162

Egesta, *see* Segesta

Elea, *see* Velia

Eleonora of Aragon, *61*

Embroidered copes, 84-6; *58, 59*

Empire style, 28, 120

Enna, 76, 80, 86, 88, 127
  Castello Lombardo, 80

Entrèves, Alessandro d', 142

Erice, 108
  Castello, *83*

Etna, 74, 75, 76, 79, 80

Exhibition architecture, 67

Exhibitionitis, 175

Ferrara, 166-7, 190
  Museo Boldini, 166-7; *142, 143*
  Palazzo dei Diamanti, 166

Florence, 50, 70-1, 154, 169-90, 192
  Accademia, 174, 184; *161, 162*
  Badia, 172, 173, 174; *147, 148*
  Baptistery, 188
  Bardini Museum, 181
  Boboli Gardens, 171
  Brancacci Chapel, 180; I
  Campanile, 182
  Castagno Museum, 181, 190
  Cathedral, 177; *154*
  Chiostro degli Aranci, *see* Badia
  Chiostro dello Scalzo, 181
  Chiostro Verde, 171, 178; *146*
  Fortezza del Belvedere, 188-90; *165*
  Horne Museum, 181; *158*
  Innocenti Pinacoteca, 181
  Museo Buonarroti, *153*
  Ognissanti, 175
  Opera del Duomo, 182; *159, 160*
  Palazzo Strozzi, 174
  Palazzo Vecchio, 173-4; *149, 150, 151, 152*

Florence, *contd.*
  Piazzale Michelangelo, 186
  Pitti, 170
  Ponte Vecchio, 50
  San Giovannino dei Cavalieri, 178; *145*
  San Lorenzo, 174
  San Miniato, 186, 188; *163, 164*
  Sant'Apollonia, *see* Castagno Museum
  Santa Maria del Carmine, 173, 180; I
  Santa Maria Novella, 174, 178; *146, 155*
  Santa Trinita, 180–1; *156, 157*
  Studiolo of Eleonora, 174; *152*
  Ufficio del Restauro, 178
  Uffizi, 170, 173, 174, 178
    Print-room, 185–6
Florence, environs of,
  San Martino alla Palma, 190–2; *166, 168*
  Villa Carducci, 190; *167*
Foce del Sele, Heraeum, 160
Fossi, Maria, 185
Framing of pictures, 44–6
Francesco di Giorgio, 46; *26*
Francis of Assisi, St, 40, 152
Francis of Paola, St, 151–2
Francis of Sales, St, 152
Francis Xavier, St, 152
Freccia del Sud, 130
Frederick II, Emperor, 48, 84, 95, 152; *98*
Fry, Roger, 72

Gaggini family, 88
Gagliardi, Rosario, 95, 96
Gardner Collection, 76
Gela, 98
Gentili, Gino Vinicio, 193
Gerace, 149–50; *127*
  Cathedral, 150; *128*
Ghirlandaio, Domenico, 174, 177
Ghirza, *117*
Giannuizzi, Pietro, 46
Gieseking, Walter, 52
Gioia Tauro, 142, 145, 149, 150
Giorgione, 38–9
Giornale di Sicilia, 70
Giovanni da Udine, 86
Girgenti, *see* Agrigento
Gissing, George, 193

Gobbo, Mario, 188
Goes, Hugo van der, 174
Goethe, Johann Wolfgang von, 95, 102, 126–8
Goldoni, Carlo, 48
Gothic art, 119, 162, 188
Gregorovius, Ferdinand, 147
Guidi, Giacomo, 82, 130, 132

Hearing and Knowing, 52
Heine, Heinrich, 95
Henraux, Lucien, 80, 96
Hermannstadt (Sibiù), 70
Hitler, Adolf, 186–8
Homer, 180
Horace, 158

Iblean hills, 90
Iesi, 46
  Palazzo del Governo, *26*
Inns, hotels and restaurants, 26, 48, 67, 73, 80,
  90, 94, 98, 108, 110–11, 113, 146, 149, 154,
  159–60
Ippari valley, 98
Isabella of Aragon, 152, 154; *131, 132*

Julius II, 27

Karnak, 34
Keats, John, 108
Klosterneuburg, 64
Kress Foundation, 166

Lacaita, Giovanni, 151
Lacaita, Sir James, 151
Laurana, Francesco, 88, 96, 106; *61, 62, 80*
Lear, Edward, 147; *125, 126, 127*
Lenormant, François, 147
Leonardo, 46
Leopardi, Giacomo, 79, 108
Leptis Magna, 130, 134–7; *111*
  Basilica of Septimius Severus, *113, 114*
  Forum of Septimius Severus, *112*
  Port, 137
  Theatre, 136; *115*
Limoges enamels, 101
Lippi, Filippino, 172, 173, 178
Lippi, Fra Filippo, 172
Locri, 144, 150; *123, 124*

Loeser Bequest, 173; *149, 150*
London, 26, 70, 146, 148
  British Museum, 145
  National Gallery, 44, 76, 152; *51*
  Westminster Bridge, 74
Longhena, Baldassare, 38, 41
Loreto, 46
  Santa Casa, *27*
Lotto, Lorenzo, 40, 42–8; *23, 24, 25*

Macerata, 48
Maganuco, Enzo, 79
Malatesta, Sigismondo, 166
Malraux, André, 52
Manfred, 95
Mantegna, Andrea, 76; *51*
Marches, 44
Marsala, 108
Marseilles, 88, 149
Masaccio, 178; *155*, I
Matisse, Henri, 178
Matteo di Giovanni, 152
Mauceri, Enrico, 70
Maxentius, 82, 83
Maximian, 82
Mazzara del Vallo, 108
  Cathedral, *84*
Melville, Herman, 140
Messina, 66–73, 74, 142
  Cathedral, 68, 120; *46*
  Church of the Catalani, 68
  Fountain of Orion, 68; *45*
  National Museum, 70
  Palazzata, 67–8; *44*
  Straights of, *43*
Michelangelo, 27, 30, 68, 86, 174, 176, 177–8,
  184, 186; *16, 153, 154, 161, 162*
Milan, 72
  Museo Poldi Pezzoli, *58*
Mileto, 148
Mino da Fiesole, 173
Modena Cathedral, 188
Modica, 96, 98
  San Giorgio, *70*
Mohammed II, 60
Mola, 74; *52*
Monaco, Lorenzo, 174, 178, 180–1; *156, 157*

Monreale, 64, 114–17, 119, 126
  Cathedral, 114–16; *92*
  Church of the Annunciation, 116–17
  Cloister of the Benedictines, *93, 94*
  Museum, 116
Monsù, 48
Montorsoli, Giovanni Angelo, 68; *45*
Morelli, Giovanni, 38
Mormanno, 158
Moses, 34; *16*
Mussolini, Benito, 50

Naples, 64, 66, 126, 140, 158, 159
  Museum, 86
  Santa Chiara, 154
Nicastro, 150
Nicholas of Verdun, 64
Noto, 95–6
  Church of the Crucifixion, 96
  Palazzo Villadorato, *68*

Odescalchi Chigi family, 28; *12*
Orlandi, Deodato, 114
Ortygia, 88
Ostia, 36
  Cardo degli Aurighi, *17*
Otranto Cathedral, 156

Paestum, 64, 111, 160
Palazzolo Acreide, 70, 88
  Chiesa dei Minori Osservanti, 88; *42, 62*
Palermo, 73, 79, 80, 85, 112, 113–28, 148; *102,
  103*
  Cappella Palatina, 64, 114; *91*
  Cathedral, 119, 126; *98, 105*
  Monte Pellegrino, 128; *104, 105*
  Municipio, 120
  National Museum (Museum of Antique Art),
  117; *61, 95, 96*
  Opera House, 124
  Oratory of San Lorenzo, 120
  Palazzo Abbatelli, 193; *97*
  Palazzo Butera, 126
  Palazzo Reale, 114; *90*
  Palazzo Sclafani, 120
  Palazzo della Zisa, 122; *101*
  Quattro Canti, 124

Palermo, contd.
  San Francesco, 120
  Villa Igea hotel, 113
Palestrina, 23, 184; *162*
  Mosaic, 31, 86
  Museum, 193; *13*
  Temple of Fortune, 7
Palinuro headland, 160
Palladian architecture, 38
Palmyra, 137
Paola, 151–2
Paris, 26, 70, 72, 118, 148, 158, 166
  Louvre, 44, 86; *25*
  Orangerie, 174
  St Denis, 60
Pater, Walter Horatio, 176, 177
Pepoli, Count Agostino, 112
Pergamon school, 178
Perugia, 80
  Cathedral, 86
  Cathedral Museum (not University), *59*
Piazza Armerina, 80, 81, 88, 193
  Environs, *see* Casale
Pienza, 85
Piero della Francesca, 71, 166
Pinturicchio, 27
Pisano, Nino, school of, 112; *87, 88*
Placci, Carlo, 80, 96
Platen, Count August von, 95, 148
Plemyrion, 90
Poggi, Giovanni, 173, 174
Policastro gulf, 159
Pollaiuolo, Antonio, 71
Pollino mountain, 156, 158
Pompeii, 25, 66
Pomposa, 167; *144*
Ponte Molle, 82
Pontormo, Jacopo da, 174
Praia a Mare, 158, 159
Procacci, Ugo, 171, 172, 190
Proust, Marcel, 170
Pythagoras of Rhegium, 142

Ragusa Ibla, 96, 98
  San Giorgio, *69*
Ramadan, Fast of, 130, 132, 138–9
Ramage, Reverend Tate, 147

Raphael, 86; *11*
Ravenna, 56, 162–4, 165, 168
  Mausoleum of Galla Placidia, 163; *138, 139*
  San Vitale, 163; III
  Sant'Apollinare in Classe, 163–4; *137*, II
  Tomb of Theodoric, 164
Regalbuto, 79
Reggio, 142–5, 149; *125*
  Angevin Castle, 142
  National Museum, 142–5; *121, 122, 123, 124*
Rembrandt, 51, 176
Renaissance art, 46, 70, 88, 119, 182
Renoir, Pierre Auguste, 33, 52
Restoration
  of architecture, 20–1
  of paintings, 172–3, 178–80
Rimini, 165–6
  Tempio Malatestiano, 119, 165–6; *140, 141*
Rivista Misena, 46
Robbia, Luca della, 182; *160*
Robert, Hubert, 36
Rococo art, 88, 96
Roger I of Sicily, 147
Roger II of Sicily, 114; *90*
Roman Campagna, 18; *3*
Romanesque art, 96, 162, 188
Rome, 17–36, 48, 50, 64, 130, 154, 158, 166
  Baths of Caracalla, 33; *15*
  Campidoglio, 30
  Central Station, 137
  Colosseum, 30
  Concordia restaurant, 26
  Forums, 30
  Monte Giordano, 26
  Museo delle Terme, 31, 33, 86, 92; *14*
  Palazzo Sacchetti, 25, 193; *8, 9*
  Palazzo Taverna, 26
  Palazzo Venezia, 34
  Pallavicini Collection, 18
  Piazza del Popolo, 26
  Piazza di Spagna, 18
  Piazza Venezia, 26
  Porta Latina, 18
  Pyramid of Cestius, 18
  Rotonda, 136
  San Giovanni in Laterano, 18
  San Lorenzo fuori le Mura, 22; *6*

San Pietro in Vincoli, 27, 34; *16*
Santa Maria in Aracoeli, 26; *10*
Santa Maria in Cosmedin, 20; *4*
Santa Maria Maggiore, 21; *5*
Santa Maria del Popolo, 27; *11, 12*
St Peter's, 24, 30; *2*
Sistine Chapel, 34
Tiber river, 26
Trinità dei Monti, 30
Vatican, 85; *2*
Via Appia, 18, 30
Via Ludovisi, 30
Via Sistina, 30
Villa di Livia, *14*
Villa di Papa Giulio, 86
Vittorio Emmanuele monument, 46
Ross, Christian, 26
Rossano Calabro, 154
   Codex Purpureus Rossanensis, 154
   San Marco, 154; *120*
   Santa Maria del Patirion, 156; *134, 136*
Rossetti, Dante Gabriel, 176
Rossi, Filippo, 170
Rudinì, Carlo di, 96
Ruskin, John, 176

Sabratha, 74, 82, 132
   Great floor mosaic, *110*
   Museum, 132
   Theatre, 132; *109*
Sacconi, Giuseppe, 46
Salviati, Francesco, 25; *9*
San Francesco del Deserto, 39; *19, 20*
Sangineto, Filippo, 154; *135*
Sankt Florian, 112
San Prisco, 64
Sansovino, Andrea, 27
Scandicci, San Martino alla Palma, 190–2; *166, 168*
Sciacca, 106; *80*
   Palazzo 'Lo Steripinto', *81*
Segesta, 64, 111–12, 113, 160; *85, 86*
Selinunte, 64, 106–8, 118; *82, 95, 96*
Selinus, *see* Selinunte
Serpotta, Giacomo, 120
Seume, Johann Gottfried, 95
Seurat, Georges, 24–5

Shelley, Percy Bysshe, 90, 108
Sibiù Museum, *48*
Siena, 80, 152
   Palazzo Tolomei, 154
Signorelli, Luca, 86
Sila plateau, 152
Sinibaldi, Giulia, 185
Spellman, Cardinal Francis Joseph, 54
Spezzano Albanese, 154
Strabo, 160
Sumerian art, 188
Sybaris, 156
Symonds, John Addington, 147
Syracuse, 64, 88–95, 130
   Achradina, 90
   Cathedral, 90, 92; *66*
   Classical Museum, *see* Museo Archaeologico
   Cyane, 90
   Epipolae, 90
   Fort of Euryelus, 90, 130
   Fort Labdalon, *63*
   Greek theatre, 90, 130
   Medieval Museum, *see* Palazzo Bellomo
   Museo Archaeologico, 90, 92; *67*
   Palazzo Bellomo, 90, 92; *65*
   Palazzo Landolino, 94
   Spring of Arethusa, 90; *64*
   Temple of Athena, 90; *66*

Tancred of Hauteville, 147
Tancredi, Tancredo, 152
Taormina, 73–6, 80; *52*
   Greek theatre, 73, 74, 75; *50*
Taranto, 151, 158
Telesio, Bernardino, 152
Terranova di Sibari, 154
Theocritus, 106
Thucydides, 74
Tiepolo, Giovanni Battista, 38
Tino di Camaino, 173; *150*
   Follower of, 154
Tintoretto, 38, 48, 51–2; *30, 31, 32*
Titian, 38, 48, 54, 56; *33*
Torcello, 56–8
   Cathedral, *34*
   Santa Fosca, *34, 35*
Trapani, 108, 110–11, 112

Trapani, *contd.*
  Museo Pepoli, 112; *89*
  Optician at, 110
  Santuario della Santissima Annunziata, 112;
    87, 88
Trescore, 43
  Oratorio Suardi, *23*
Tripoli, 130–2, 137–40
  Arch of Marcus Aurelius, 137; *116*
  Castello, 139–40; *106, 117, 118, 119*
  Lungomare, 130
  Museum, *see* Castello
  Oasis of Tagiura, 140
  Saniet Volpi, 130–2; *107, 108*

Uccello, Paolo, 171, 178, 188; *146, 163*
Udine, 159
Urbino, 88

Vallo di Lucania, 159
Vallombrosa, 162
Vasari, Giorgio, 188
Veblen, Thorstein, 53
Vecchietta, 27
Velasquez, 160
Velia, 160
Veneziani, Cavaliere, 82
Venice, 37–64, 72, 168
  Accademia, 64; *40*
  Campo San Moisè, 48; *28, 29*
  Correr, 70, 71
  Dogana, 52
  Doge's Palace, 53, 60
  Fenice, 52
  Gesuiti, 56; *33*
  Giorgio Cini Foundation, *see* San Giorgio
    Maggiore

Grand Canal, 48, 60
  Lagoon of, *19, 20, 34, 35*
  Pala d'Oro, 64; *41*
  Piazza, 52, 60
  Piazzetta, 52, 60
  San Cassiano, 72
  San Giorgio Maggiore, 41–2, 53; *21, 22*
  San Marco, 54, 58–64; *18, 36, 37, 38, 39, 40,
    41*
  Scuola di San Rocco, 51; *30, 31, 32*
Verga, Giovanni, 78
Vergara Caffarelli, Ernesto, 132, 134, 136, 139;
  111
Veronese, Paolo, 38
Victor Emmanuel III, 108
Villa San Giovanni, 66
Virgil, 106
Vittoria, 95, 98
  Madonna delle Grazie, *71*
  Public gardens, 98
  Teatro Comunale, *71*
Volpi, Giuseppe, 130

Wanderlust, 75
Washington, D.C., 70, 73, 175
Watteau, Antoine, 20
Whistler, James Abbott McNeill, 56
Wharton, Edith Newbold, 78
William II of Sicily, *94*
Willmore, Arthur, *73*
Wordsworth, William, 74
Wright, Frank Lloyd, 48

Xenodochiophobia, 66

Zanotti Bianco, 160
Zampetti, Pietro, 40